Hell of A Way to Run a Railroad

By Joe Harris

Order this book online at www.trafford.com
or email orders@trafford.com

Most Trafford titles are also available at major online book retailers.

Note for Librarians: A cataloguing record for this book is available from Library
and Archives Canada at www.collectionscanada.ca/amicus/index-e.html

Printed in Victoria, BC, Canada.

ISBN: 978-1-4269-1476-8 (Soft)
ISBN: 978-1-4269-1477-5 (Hard)

Library of Congress Control Number 2009933019

*We at Trafford believe that it is the responsibility of us all, as both individuals
and corporations, to make choices that are environmentally and socially sound.
You, in turn, are supporting this responsible conduct each time you purchase a
Trafford book, or make use of our publishing services. To find out how you are
helping, please visit www.trafford.com/responsiblepublishing.html*

*Our mission is to efficiently provide the world's finest, most comprehensive
book publishing service, enabling every author to experience success.
To find out how to publish your book, your way, and have it available
worldwide, visit us online at www.trafford.com*

Trafford rev. 9/14/2009

www.trafford.com

North America & international
toll-free: 1 888 232 4444 (USA & Canada)
phone: 250 383 6864 ♦ fax: 812 355 4082 ♦ email: info@trafford.com

Table of Contents

Dedication

In memory of my parents,
Joseph T. Harris, Sr. and Leola Lois Harris

Preface

I regret that I did not get interest in my English and History courses in high school until my senior year. After a long career on the railroad, I decided to write a book about it. I went to college after I retired to brush up on all the skills needed to perform this task.

I want to thank my professors at Rowan Cabarrus Community College for giving me the knowledge for this endeavor. To Donna Ginn, in particular, agreeing to help me proof the pages for errors in grammar and punctuation. Word documents could only help me so much.

For Bonnie, my wife, for assisting me and giving me encouragement, to Tom Graham, a lifelong friend and my brother Len, helping me plan and build my house. Also, to my daughter Peggy and George Mekebak for their endless hours helping me to clear the property of dead trees and turning the lot into a park.

To my friends and family who have given me encouragement in life as well as this book, I thank you very much.

There are a lot of people who do not know about railroading and the terminology associated with it. Some of these people are in the newspaper and news media business. I hope this book will enlighten those and others who want to know a little more about the industry.

Chapter One-The Early Years

In order to explain how I got into railroading, I have to go back to my childhood. I was born January 26, 1945 in Fayetteville, North Carolina. My father was a heavy equipment operator similar to the job he had in the Navy in World War II; they were called Seabees. The Seabees were the first people on land to build roads and airstrips. My father was also a carpenter and introduced me into building houses.

My mother worked in banks, as a secretary, and in other jobs. My older brothers told me I ran around the house naked when I was around two or three; I later found out why. There was a pot of water on the heater in the living room in the house where we lived. I apparently pulled the handle of the pot and the hot water scolded my body. So to keep the medicine on my body, mom didn't put any clothes on me.

Both of my parents worked, and often times we were not supervised; that is not good when you have three boys ranging from 5 to 9 years old. On one occasion Lonnie and David, my two older brothers, skipped school and went down to the creek we called River Rouge in Detroit, Michigan. There was barge that a construction crew was using for mixing concrete that Lonnie thought would be a great boat. They put the barge into the water and got into it and were sailing away from the bank when it began to sink. They started yelling and yelling and attracted the attention of the police who were at a nearby shooting range. There went the secret of them skipping school! Lonnie was punished really tough that night.

My brother, David, was a firebug; he loved starting fires and watching them. One day he was striking matches and throwing them into a container of gasoline and then backing off. After three attempts with the same result, he struck a match and threw it in the container and stood there to watch it. Sure enough, it blew up that time and set his face on fire. David went into the house and was washing his face when the babysitter came in and saw him. She knew it was strange, a boy that age washing his face without being told. When they went to the doctor, the doctor told my parents that washing his face with water was best thing he could have done at the time.

Another time David was putting a stick inside the wood stove and after getting the tip red hot would take it out and make smoke rings with it. My grandmother came in about that time, so he stuck the burning stick into his shirt to hide it. As grandmother was talking to him, she noticed his shirt begin to smoke. Grandmother got the stick out and today he still has a fifty-cent piece size scar on his chest where he was burned.

When we were at Uncle George's house one time, my brother Lonnie convinced our cousin, Marion, to put his arm into the washing machine ringer. The ringer pulled Marion's arm all the way up to his shoulder into the ringer. One of the boys ran to the front porch where mom and Aunt Minnie were talking and was trying to tell them about Marion being stuck in the washer. Mom told him not to interrupt them. Finally, he blurted out that Marion was struck, and they both got up and ran to the back porch to rescue Marion.

We loved to climb trees at Uncle George's house. One day, my sister, Jeanette, and I were climbing trees, and she fell out of the tree and broke her arm. Another time she fell out and landed on a sharp stump on her hip. I saw the blood coming from her hip, and I ran into the house tell the adults. Jeanette had to be taken to the hospital to get stitches.

In my early days we didn't have four rooms and a bath; it was four rooms and a "path." I always had a fear of falling into one of those holes in the "outhouse." One of my cousins did fall in the open hole of the outhouse one day. She survived, but I think I would have died of embarrassment.

In 1950 we moved to Detroit, Michigan. At that time there were five of us children- Lonnie, the oldest, David Leroy, myself, Jeannette, the only girl in the family, besides Mom of course, and Colon Mintz, whom we called Butch. Later on there were two other children born, Len Edward and James. That made a total of seven children born to my parents. James, the youngest brother, was born one weekend I had liberty while I was in the Navy in Norfolk, Virginia.

We went to church at Temple Baptist Church on Grand Rivers Avenue in Detroit, Michigan. The church had the largest Sunday school in the world at that time. Instead of stairs going up and down to different levels, they had ramps. I remember as a young boy, I used to have fun running up and down the ramps, and naturally I was always scolded for that.

We hated cleaning up like most children do, and we tried to make quick work of it so we could go play. Jeanette and I thought after sweeping the trash up into a pile, we wouldn't have to pick the trash up, if we just sweep the trash down the vent nicely located on the floor. The bad thing was it was the heating vent. Because of the trash we swept down the vents, we had a fire one Thanksgiving, and the fire department had to put the fire out that had started in walls.

One Christmas Lonnie and David got a bicycle and Jeanette and I received a red wagon. I really wanted a bike also, but I guess it's a good thing I didn't get one. I borrowed a bike from a friend and was riding it, but with my inexperience, I drove right into a tree. I slipped off the seat and cut my privates on the handlebars. It was very embarrassing to have my pants down, and have my mother and Aunt Minnie, a nurse, check my scrotum to access the cut I had received for the accident.

On summer vacations to Fayetteville, North Carolina, my parents farmed us out to other relatives for visitations and sleeping arrangements. My parents owned a 1953 Hudson at the time and I remember sleeping in the floor board in the back. My sister, Jeanette, was small enough to sleep in the back glass. My grandparents, James and Betty Harris, lived in the country of Cumberland County, North Carolina. I remember some of the nights I would lay in bed and hear the Atlantic Coast Line train with the engineer blowing the whistle of the train going toward Clinton, North Carolina in the eastern part of the state. Looking out the window, I could see the oscillating light of the engine lighting up the horizon. Although a lot of children want to grow up to be an engineer of a train, I never dreamed that I would eventually become a locomotive engineer.

In 1958, hurricane Hazel hit Cumberland County. The winds were quite terrific, and subsequently blew over a great big oak tree that was about 3 feet in diameter near our back porch at grandmother's house.

Fortunately, it fell away from the porch and caused no damage to the house. It was amazing though, gathering together in that small house through all of those high winds; we survived without having even a scratch.

It was on another one of my visits that my grandfather died in the outhouse. Apparently there is a name for that, the strain of going to the bathroom and having a fatal heart attack. I saw him fall out of the outhouse, and I ran to my grandmother to tell her. She told me to run to the neighbor's house for help, as we had no telephone. She told me not to run, for I had rheumatic fever when I was younger, but I ran like the wind. However, nothing could save my grandpa's life.

We moved from Detroit, Michigan back to Fayetteville, North Carolina in 1958. I attended Massey Hill School in Fayetteville, NC. I completed sixth and seven grades at this school. When we moved to Vander, North Carolina, I was in the eighth grade at Stedman High School.

I went to high school at Stedman High School in Stedman, NC until the twelfth grade. I remember often times my friend, Freddy Hall, and I thumbed our way to school. We also thumbed for rides going back home. One time during the summer, Freddy and I thumbed our way to Wilmington, North Carolina to the beach. When we were thumbing back home, the highways were so deserted and not much traffic, we slept on the side of the road leaning up against a tree. One day Freddy and I was playing around with Jeanette. Freddy had an arm and a leg, and I had her other arm and leg and we were busting her butt up against the sheetrock wall. We must have gotten too serious, for we busted a hole in the sheetrock. We had to think fast, so we rearranged the living room furniture to cover the hole before mom and dad got back home from work. When mom came home, she was really impressed that we rearranged the furniture on our own. It was not until I went into the Navy that Mom found out what happened.

One day, Freddy and I "borrowed" my brother's 1955 Oldsmobile. We pushed it out of the driveway and down the street a little way, and then we started it up so nobody could hear us. We picked up a couple more of our friends, and then went cruising around town. When we came back home, we eased into the driveway so nobody would know we were at home. Although no one said anything, I do not think we got away with it.

My dad and I had some words between us after I skipped school one day, and I ran away from home. I was thumbing a ride on Road 74 near Raeford, NC heading toward Charlotte, North Carolina. With no traffic in sight at 9:30 pm, I decided to thumb a ride and go back to Fayetteville, NC. I went to my Aunt Marie's house in Massey Hill and asked her if I could live there and go to school at Massey Hill High School. She said I could, so I transferred and finished high school there. I didn't know until later, my dad had paid Aunt Marie for me to live there.

In the sixties, we had to register for the draft, so that is what I did. We had to take a hearing test and a physical to see if we were healthy enough to go into the military. There was a story of one fellow draftee who didn't want to go into the military, so he was making like he didn't hear while he was in the soundproof booth. Outside the booth, the knobs were adjusted and he was asked again; "Can you hear me?" The guy didn't say or do anything. She adjusted the knobs again and said, "Can you hear me now?" Again he didn't do anything. Then she said, "If you can't hear me, take the earphone off and put it on the other ear!" So he took the phone off and put it on the other ear. My fellow draftee fell for that.

There was a group of people standing in two lines facing each other. The doctor had a sense of humor; he had everyone turn around and strip naked. Then he told them to bend over and spread their cheeks. When you did that, you were looking at all the other butts across the room. We had to give a urine sample so they gave you a bottle, and told us to go in the bathroom to fill it up. My friend couldn't go, so he looked over at the guy next to him that had a good stream going into the urinal, and asked him to fill his bottle also.

Chapter Two- You're in the Navy Now

Having seen enough of Army green at Fort Bragg, North Carolina and not wanting to be drafted, after graduating from high school in 1963 from Massey Hill High School, I decided to join the U.S. Navy like my dad. The female members of the Navy were called waves. There was a saying in the Navy – I joined the Navy to ride the waves, but all I did was go to sea.

After basic training at the Great Lakes Naval Training Station, I was stationed in Providence, Rhode Island for Quartermaster school. The wind from the bay would chill me to the bone when I walked in the open areas from the bunkhouse to the mess hall. I was in class in Quartermaster school when we were informed that President John F. Kennedy was killed. It was and still is very unbelievable.

After Quartermaster school, I was assigned to the USS Fremont APA-44 in Norfolk, Virginia. The USS Fremont was a troop transport in the Sixth Fleet. The ship could carry 1200 combat-ready marines. The Fremont was in the movie "The Longest Day" as one of the support ships. We carried the U.S. Marines from Morehead City, North Carolina to cruises in the _ and Caribbean Sea.

While in the Navy, I had a chance to see more of the world than I would have otherwise. I was not on the ship very long before I made my first Mediterranean Sea cruise. The first port we visited was Valetta, Malta. Valetta was established in 1500s. The city was comprised of limestone buildings.

In 1964, while on liberty in Valetta, Malta, I went into a club that had pictures of a new singing group with long hair, compared to our military haircut, and I wondered if they would make a lasting impression on the music industry. I remembered we made several remarks about their looks. I think they did pretty well for themselves, the group was the Beatles.

In the "Cyprus" crisis that same year our ship had to steam 125 miles southwest of the Island of Crete and standby in case we had to drop our Marines off to assist in any way. We were at sea for two months without seeing land. We pulled liberty on the USS Enterprise, an aircraft carrier. That was a big ship. The big "E" as we called it.

On one of my liberties from Norfolk, I went to see my parents. While Dad and I were talking in the living room, I had to ask him a question that was burning in my head for years. I asked why being the third son born I was named Junior after him, Joseph T. Harris, Jr. He said, "You were born while I was ten days at sea going to the Philippines in World War II. Your mother asked me before I left what should she name the child. I replied if it's a girl, name her after you, and if it's a boy, name him after me." I never questioned being called Junior again, because I could have been named "Leola Lois."

The quartermasters steered the ship on special occasions like going into and out of ports and highline. Highline was when two ships got close enough to each other to transfer mail, food or people across from one ship to another. When the ships were that close to each other we couldn't vary in either direction at all for you would run into the other ship.

In the pilothouse, the Quartermaster had a desk to keep records of the ships log. Near that desk was a 300 pound safe. On one cruise, the weather was abnormally rough and the motion of the waves sent that safe across the pilothouse. The captain had it welded to the deck the next day. Right behind the pilothouse was the navigator's room where we had all our charts for the seas that we went to. A fellow seaman, Larry Swope, was a lithographer. When we had to lay down new tile in the pilothouse, he engraved a sextant in a different color tile on the floor. It sure did look good. A sextant is a navigational instrument incorporating a telescope and an angular scale that is used to work out latitude and longitude. We used this instrument to get bearings of the sun, moon, and stars, so we would know where we were anywhere in the ocean.

I met a couple of good friends while serving in navy, James Roberts from Birmingham, Alabama and Rodger Scolfield from Pensacola,

Florida. We went on liberty together and worked together around on the ship. I ran into another sailor who became a friend. I was walking up the ladder (stairway) to the main deck and he was coming down. So we basically ran into each other. His name was David Cornell. I went up to Stephentown, New York where he lived, and I went out on a date with his sister. I also pulled liberty in Alabama with Roberts ("Tank" as we called him). I also went to visit him later after I was on the railroad. He had become a truck driver.

I would always kid with my fellow sailors about letters I got from back home. I told them my mom wrote to me and said, "I'm writing this letter slow, son, because I know you don't read too fast. I would have sent the $20 you asked for, but I didn't think about it until after I sealed the envelope."

I wrote to her one day and said, "I sure do appreciate the way you raised me and taught me table manners, because some of these guys would shock you with their table manners. Why just the other day I saw this guy eating green peas with a knife. It shocked me so bad that I dropped a handful of mashed potatoes."

I never did get sea sick, although some of the seas were quite rough. I was a quartermaster, which was in the navigation division. In the Army, a quartermaster is a person that issues out supplies and uniforms, but in the Navy a quartermaster is a navigator. At quartermaster school, we were taught how to read charts which are maps for bodies of water, navigate by the sun and stars, and how to read a compass. Three bearings to known locations of landmarks would give us a relative bearing of our exact position in the water.

We went from Norfolk, Virginia to the Mediterranean Sea. The trip took 12 days to cross the Atlantic Ocean. At the mouth of the Mediterranean Sea was the Rock of Gibraltar. There was a lighthouse on the rock for navigators to use as a landmark. In every port were buoys to mark the channel. Red buoys were on the right and green buoys were on the left as we entered into port. We had a saying to remember about the color of the buoys which was, "Red right, returning from sea."

Buoys and lighthouses had different flashing light patterns, so we could distinguish them from each another. We would have to get the bearings from these objects, so we could know where we were in the ocean. Now, the ships have global positioning satellites. At the push of a button, the ships will know where they are within three feet in the ocean.

The following is the history of the USS Fremont pulled off the web site USS Fremont: http://www.ussfremont.org/frewin/html

1964- The beginning of a new year found Fremont deployed to the Mediterranean. While in the Mediterranean, the Cyprus Crisis erupted and the ship and its task force spent three months navigating around "Point Cirrus"(125 miles SE of Crete)on standby to go in and evacuate NATO personnel from Cyprus. The following is a personal observation of LCDR David W. Fowler who was a DT2 at the time: "I well remember entering Malta in Mar 64 after some 74 days at sea. The ship's party in Barcelona was held in a club with a "house of ill repute' on the second level. The Commodore was most perplexed when a lovely 'hooker' sat on his lap." The first break from this drudgery was on St Patrick's Day when the USS Enterprise and her task force put on an air show. The first liberty port was Valletta, Malta in April; Naples, Italy twice; and Barcelona, Spain as Fremont worked her way out of the Med. The last Mediterranean stop was Majorca but the ship's crew did not pull liberty. Amphibious landings were conducted in Turkey, Sardinia, and Corsica with NATO Forces.

During the June to September period, Fremont operated out of Little Creek and NOB Norfolk and did make one trip to the Camp LeJeune area to put the Marines on the beach.

On 14 August 1964, Captain Charles K. Schmidt, USN assumed command of Fremont from Captain Julian T. Burke, USN. Following Captain Schmitt's assuming command, Fremont deployed the end of September to the Caribbean. The deployment gave Fremont the opportunity to train her new personnel in their duties concerning amphibious warfare. An interesting sidelight to the deployment was the transfer of 200 four and 1/2 ton baulks from Guantanamo Bay, Cuba to San Juan, Puerto Rico where they were used as camels for the ships in that area. The baulks were loaded on hatches and any other deck space that was available. It was quite an engineering feat as well as a peculiar sight to see the baulks loaded aboard. The transporting of the baulks was a true exhibition of the Fremont's versatility. During the cruise, Fremont spent a lot of time off of and landing on Isle De Vieques where the Marines were based. Ports of call were Ponce, Puerto Rico; St. Thomas, St Croix, and Curacao in the Netherlands Antilles.

The Caribbean cruise was a lot nicer than the previous Mediterranean cruise.

1965-Fremont departed the Caribbean and returned to her home port on 22 January. The return home was eagerly anticipated, but the cold weather encountered was not and many of the crew members longed to return to the warm weather they had just left. From 22 January until 2 June, USS Fremont remained in her home port taking advantage of the time to send many members of the crew to various schools for training. Groups of reservists came aboard for two 2 week periods and were treated to exhibitions of the duties of an APA, including many General Quarters and "2-ALFAS". (Yebba n.d.)

On 2 June, Fremont departed her home part for a 5 month tour of duty with the Sixth Fleet in the Mediterranean with BIT 2/2 embarked. Five specialized troop landings were conducted during the cruise. The major landing saw Fremont land troops on the shore of Greece in a NATO operation. The operation gave Fremont and her crew a chance to work with members of the Greek Services and identify the problems involved with the different techniques employed by foreign nations.

On 30 June, while in the Spanish port of Valencia, members of Fremont's rescue and assistance detail were instrumental in saving the Spanish oceanographic Ship XAUEN, from destruction by fire. The detail, answering a plea for assistance from the ship, spent about one and one-half hours combating the blaze. The commanding officer of the stricken ship sent a letter of appreciation to Fremont for her help.

Fremont also held a 4th of July party for some 200 American residents while in Valencia. The celebration was carried out in the traditional manner with band music from Fremont's "pop music" combo, hot dogs and hamburgers, boxing matches, and a starlight movie on the main deck. A fine time was enjoyed by all.

On 24 August while in Genoa, Italy, Fremont welcomed aboard a new commanding officer, Captain Martin M. Casey Jr., USN, who relieved Captain Charles K. Schmidt, USN.

Members of the ship's basketball and baseball teams were given special recognition while in Valletta, Malta during the period 9-17 September for winning the squadron tournaments. While in Valletta, Fremont crew members "pitched in" and helped renovate the grounds of Begija orphanage in Hemrun, a suburb of Valletta. The crew assisted in painting fences and benches, and the installation of outdoor lighting.

They also presented the orphanage with a brightly decorated table and set of chairs manufactured onboard Fremont. During the renovation activities, the Fremont's "combo" entertained the children while cake and soft drinks were served.

On 21 October Fremont departed the Mediterranean and returned home to Norfolk on 3 November. Sea duty for the year not yet completed, Fremont got underway again on 6 December to accomplish many of the required exercises for the fiscal year and to conduct training in the ship to shore movement exercise. During this period, liberty was enjoyed for a weekend visit to New York City on 10 December.

Fremont returned to Norfolk on 17 December for a holiday upkeep period. Many of the crew took advantage of this period to spend the holiday at home with family and friends.

1966-During the first months of 1966, Fremont alternated between local operations and in-port upkeep periods in Norfolk.

The 1st major event of the year was the change of command for PHIBRON 4. On 6 April, Captain R. S. Salter USN relieved Captain Neal Almgren as Squadron Commander aboard Fremont. Although the squadron staff was quartered ashore, Fremont was selected as the site for the ceremony, since the ship had recently been the Commodore's Flagship during the Mediterranean deployment. It was at this time that I attended survival school in Norfolk, Virginia to prepare to go to Vietnam.

After serving on the USS Fremont (APA-44) for two and one-half years, I received orders for Da-Nang, Vietnam, where I served as Quartermaster (QM1) on a yard craft utility. That was a craft that could carry 100 tons of cargo to supply the troops near the DMZ in North Vietnam. The amphibious fleet was called gators. The headquarters in Danang, Vietnam was called the White Elephant. We had a gator painted on our pilothouse with a screw in his belly. We wanted to paint a white elephant holding a screwdriver in front of the gator, but we thought that would get us in too much trouble.

As a quartermaster, I had to learn the Morse code to communicate with other ships through light and semaphore system. A semaphore system communicates letters by the position of our arms with flags in our hands. In Vietnam, we limited radio communication and used light signals to communicate with other ships. As an E-5 petty officer, I was one of the petty officers of the deck. When I was on duty as petty officer, I had to wear the standard issue 45-caliber pistol.

On one occasion while I was petty officer, I had several boats with Vietnamese children gathering around the boat begging for food. I was trying to shoo them away from the craft, and having no luck doing that, I pulled out my weapon. I released the clip and put it in my pocket. I pointed the gun at a little girl in the boat to scare her off. When the boats did not leave, I started applying and pressure to the trigger, pointing the gun at this little girl's head. I was just trying to scare her off, and then I remembered there could be a bullet in the chamber. Sure enough, I pulled the release of the gun back and ejected a bullet out of the chamber. I still have bad dreams about that, about how close I came to shooting this girl.

It was in Vietnam that I picked up playing the guitar. We could buy a guitar for $10, but if you broke a guitar string, you had to buy another guitar to replace the string, as strings were not available. I went through three guitars in one year. A fellow sailor, Alonzo Payne, from Indianapolis, Indiana, and I played the guitar as much as we could to kill time while we were over there with nothing else to do. My fingertips were very tough from playing the guitar that long. The normal "uniform–of–the–day" was a bathing suit and shower shoes. One day I was sitting in a chair resting when another one of my friends (Michael Schwab) came up to me and put a wad of chewing gum in my belly button. The gum stuck to my hair and was a mess to pull and cut out. He didn't know what trouble that gum caused, and I didn't leave him alone until I returned the "favor."

We carried anything from two tanks to 100 tons of Coca-Cola for the two cities that we traveled to. Thank goodness, I never had confrontations with the enemy, but we did have a couple of scary moments. We always sailed at night to arrive in the city by morning. One night we were having a hard time trying to find where we were on the coast in the South China Sea. That night our petty officer told our "Skipper" we were okay, but I finally convinced the skipper that we were north of the DMZ and had overshot the mouth of the river to Dong Ho by four miles. I was quite relieved to get back "south" of the DMZ.

One night while we were anchored in the harbor, a couple friends and I swam to shore to party. We had to swim about 100 yards to shore and then walk along the road in the darkness to find "the action."

Afterwards, we had to swim back to the ship. Thinking about it later, I felt that was a real dumb thing to do. The reason is because the people we ran into could have been the enemy. That was not smart-not smart at all.

While over in Vietnam, we were allowed a five-day pass to various places; I went to Tokyo, Japan. I really liked it there and was planning to go back, but never did. It was quite an interesting experiencing the different cooking styles of Japan and the USA. I spent five days in Tokyo, Japan and I enjoyed it very much. Of course, the nightly routines were going to the bars, drinking and having a good time. That liberty was a welcome, relaxing time away from Vietnam. The time I spent in Tokyo was way too short.

Everyone looked forward to the time when it was their time to go back home to the states. Well, would you believe when it was my time to go home, I came down with a fever and the doctor was worried that I may have had malaria? I was half delirious when the nurse was trying to get a finger prick to get blood for a smear to check for malaria. He was jabbing the tip of my finger to get blood and then "milking it," but could not get any blood to flow out of my finger.

Finally, I realized what was going on so I told him to try my other hand as I had been playing the guitar and probably couldn't get through the callus on my finger. As soon as he tried my other hand, he got his blood right away. Anyway, I was stuck in sickbay until my fever went down, and was well enough to travel. After I recovered from the fever, I got my turn on the plane to go "stateside" to Clark Air Force base to get discharged. Everyone said they would kiss the ground when they got off the plane in the "states", but I actually did it. I was glad to be back at home.

When I was at Clark Air Force base to get discharged, I met a guy named Helmut Volkenhuber. He was from Philadelphia, Pennsylvania. Yes, that is his real name. He was a German with citizenship papers and he was being discharged a couple of days before I was to be discharged. Helmut and I became friends and decided to go to St. Louis, Missouri to see a girl he had been writing while he was in Vietnam. We were going to travel on Route 66 just like on the TV show.

The trip was quite fun, perhaps because of the first taste of freedom or that we just got along and had fun. We slept in the car at night and drove in the daytime. It was a bust with his pen pal in St. Louis, so we went to Burlington, Iowa. Helmut and I were cruising around the streets of Burlington in his 1958 Mercury when we drove by the YWCA. There were several girls sitting on the front steps when we came by and waved at them. A couple of them waved back, so we went around the block and saw them again. We waved, and they waved back.

The third time around the block we stopped and all but two of the girls scurried into the building. We introduced ourselves, to them and one of them was Pamela Welch. Helmut's girl didn't work out, but Pam and I got along.

Chapter Three – Work, Work, Work

Pam and I got along well enough, in fact, to get married. I really did have a good relationship with my father-in-law, Gordon Welch. As Pam and I got into the car to go on our honeymoon, Gordon yelled out to Pam, "Keep your legs crossed." He was a real funny character. We went to bars and played pool together. He was a real good friend to me.

He had a real good sense of humor, and I guess I got a lot of my smart-butt ways from him. Gordon was a go-getter. He was working a swing shift at an electro-generator plant on the Mississippi River, worked part time at a service station, plus he bought and sold cars since he had a lot of knowledge about them.

The first apartment that Pam and I had was a one-room apartment with two doors inside the room. One door led to a closet and the other door led to the bathroom. Inside the room were a bed, a table with chairs, and a kitchen. All the comforts of home, yeah right!

The money you received from the Navy, when discharged, just doesn't last long, so it wasn't too long before we had to get real jobs to substantiate our fun. Helmut and I got jobs at an antennae factory. Bending tubing was not a fun job, and it didn't last long. My brother, David, moved from Fayetteville, North Carolina to live in Burlington, Iowa, and he got a job at US Gypsum Company. Not long from that antennae job, I went to US Gypsum making sheetrock where my brother David had a job. I worked there about a year before moving on. I started out at "face" where you inspected the sheetrock coming out of the kiln. I moved up to the knife where the sheetrock was cut before going into the kiln to dry. I finished up at the "machine" where the sheetrock was in the slurry state. I had to keep the sheetrock from hardening on the corners of the machine so the hardened slurry wouldn't cut the paper.

Pam and I had a baby boy on August 31, 1968, and we named him after me, Joseph T. Harris, III. Peggy Sue was born later in 1971 in Aurora, Illinois.

Now comes the part you have been waiting for. I was hired out at the Burlington Shops in Burlington, Iowa on the CB&Q which stands for Chicago, Burlington, and Quincy. I was an electrician's helper. It was a 7am to 3pm inside job that basically had me cleaning electrical parts of traction motors off of locomotives. These shops rebuilt the parts of the locomotive and put them back in the locomotive. I lived right across the road from the shops, so I walked to work, and I came home for lunch at noon, where Pam had lunch made (soup and sandwich).

With the increasing demands of a family, I was also working in a cookie factory in Burlington, Iowa to make more money. I worked the wrapping machine at that plant. On the weekends, I was also working at a service station pumping gas. It really doesn't take too long to get tired during the week when you allow yourself no time to rest. I was as they say "burning the candle at both ends", so I started weeding out jobs, so I could get some rest.

There were a bunch of "smart butts" at the Burlington shops so there was never a dull moment. We were always pulling pranks on one another. We used a jelly substance that was called bluing, and it was used for lubrication in the traction motors somehow. If I got this jell on my hands, it would stain them so bad I had to wear it off. There was a guy named Graper who always tried to stay clean and immaculate. So, we put this bluing on an electrode that he had to handle, and sure enough he got it all over his hands.

If anyone came down the aisles at work that was "new," we always whistled at them and then turn around acting like we were working. We had little wooden stools that we sat on for breaks and lunch that were painted red. The same bright red paint that we insulated the traction motors with. If I were not very observant, Hillary Myers would paint those seats just before break so when I came and sat down on them, I would have a bright red butt and everyone would know I had been sitting down. One day I came back to sit down on one of those seats I didn't know Hillary had just painted. I sat on the stool and I got paint all over my pants. I didn't know to what extent until I got home and found red paint all the way down to my underwear. I had it on my skin through all of my clothes.

Everyone who started working in the shops started working with Hillary, so it was not a surprise when people always came back to our area to visit. One such fellow was a crane operator who always brought his lunch bucket to our area and put it down, because it was in the path between the time card clock and the exit.

Now, if you don't believe the dead come back to life, just watch that place at quitting time. When he placed his lunch bucket down and left to clock out, Hillary and I loaded the lunch bucket up with heavy metal and bolts. The lunch bucket probably weighed 30 pounds. After clocking out, he came around the corner of the aisle heading for the exit at a high rate of speed. When he grabbed his lunch bucket by the handle on the fly, only the handle came up. The lunch bucket with the metal stayed on the floor.

I had a friend named Jonathan in the shops and he bought a motorboat. One day as our families went on a picnic, the night fell on us quickly and we had to navigate up the "Mighty Mississippi" in the dark. My Navy experience proved worthy as we came alongside of several large ships using the river with barges. I knew Jonathan and I were a little scared going in and about those large ships with our tiny boat.

One individual at the shops gave me insight for the rest of my career; I was griping about how incompetent the railroad is and failure to make what I thought was better decisions. He told me this, "Son, if you don't like the way the railroad is going now, then you better get out while you're ahead, because it's never going to change." I found that to be very true in the years that followed on the railroad.

I had a neighbor that had a model train set and I helped him with it. This was my first experience with a model train and I thought it was cool. The only bad problem was the size of the nails. I had to use tweezers to hold them, because they were so small for my fat fingers. Model railroading was a hobby that I myself started later. It was a lot of fun laying out the tracks. Placing tracks and forming your own railroad was quite interesting. In the later years, building my railroad train set, I built more and more complex wiring, so I had to learn how to eliminate shorts in the wiring. I was eventually able to operate the trains without creating a dead short.

Someone at the shops told me that the brakemen on the CB&Q make more money than we did in the shops. I learned that the CB&Q were hiring brakemen in Aurora, Illinois. I thought about it and decided I should transfer to that part of railroading. I asked the superintendent of the shops for a transfer and he granted it. When I was leaving the shop for the last time, he gave me a bit of advice that I tried to live by. He said, "Son, you have to blow your own horn, nobody's going to blow it for you."

The training I received when the trainmaster hired me as a brakeman sure did lack by today's standard. He showed me how to tie a hand brake on a boxcar, couple an air hose, and use the angle cock to cut in the air. He gave me a lantern and a switch key and I was called for third shift that night. The first two people I worked with were called Haggy and Hogie. One was the yard foreman and the other was the switchman. I was totally lost and I felt like a dummy, because I didn't pick up on the aspects of the job as quickly as I wanted. Railroading is a different job because of the different things you have to do. It doesn't require a lot of strength, but common sense is definitely a plus.

It was in the Enola Yard in Chicago, Illinois that night that I started learning the job of brakeman. It's was hard for me to learn what's going on when I was in the middle of nowhere with nothing but a dim bulb in a lantern to light my way. We had a pretty neat system to signal the engineer on the engine. The yard had a green, yellow, and red light suspended on a pole 30 feet tall. The engineer could see these lights around the long curve of the track. The switches to operate these lights were in a little shanty. If I wanted the engineer to move toward you slowly, I would turn on the yellow light. If I wanted to kick a car faster, I would turn on the green light. And naturally, if I wanted the engineer to stop, I would turn on the red light. The other switchmen would signal to me and I would operate the lights for the engineer to move.

Working in the yard has never been one of my favorite jobs because the train would just go backwards and forward, back and forth, back and forth; you get the idea. I liked being "on the road" for I seemed to have a sense of accomplishment by completing a run. I didn't stay on the yard long before I set my sights on the main line.

With my seniority, the only job I could hold was in passenger service. I remember the train number was 25, and I made $25 a day for the assignment. The train started out of Chicago, Illinois and went to Savanna, Illinois a total of 125 miles; it didn't take long to go that distance. Of course, we made passenger stops along the way.

When we got off the train in Savanna, we went to a boarding house where we "took rest" to be ready to go back on the train back to Chicago. There was a book we had to sign in like a register book, and I thought it was curious to be in a boarding house rather than a hotel. There was no talk between the "old heads" and the new people, I just followed them like a little puppy dog and tried to learn. They didn't want to share their knowledge with me. Afraid I would know as much as they did, I guess.

Maybe I could have learned quicker if someone took the effort to take me under their wing and help me understand, but that was the exception rather the rule. So in the long run, I just learned as I worked through the different jobs.

It didn't take long to get tired of both the pay and the job on the passenger train, so I changed to be a collector on the commuter trains that ran from Aurora, Illinois to Chicago, Illinois, and a total of 34 miles. The people who worked in Chicago found commuter trains to be an alternate way to travel to the big city. We went through towns like Naperville, Downers Grove and Cicero. There were three main line tracks with the commuter trains going through the crossovers and the towns in rapid fashion.

Early in the morning there was a "parade of trains going into Chicago, Illinois" and in the afternoon the "parade" came back going to Aurora, Illinois. Both the passenger train and the commuter train required the collectors and conductors to be in uniform. I sold tickets in the passenger cars as the train sped between stations. I had a pocket full of tickets and a coin changer to give back change. While on duty, the action was fast paced until you arrived into the terminal. After the train arrived at the station, we went into the depth of Union Station where the crew's room was located.

One of the duties of a ticket collector was to back the train from the coach yard, where the trains are parked when not in use. The trains were kept at the coach yard until it was time to get the train into Union Station, ready for the afternoon rush hour. The trainman had a backup hose to apply the air brakes when the train got closer to the bumping block. Some of the switches were called puzzle switches for good reason. I had to look carefully at the way I was going to make sure I was going on the right track and direction. Some of the switches could move the train on multiple routes and that was why they were called puzzle switches. After parking the train, the trainman took the backup hose off and stood by the train to answer all the questions that were sure to be forthcoming.

Some of the older guys went to the stock market and worked as pages while off duty. Others just read, napped or rested for the next run. In some of those days, I took my guitar to make the time go quicker. One of the young collectors that I worked with played the harmonica, so we played together. It was one of those times that we messed up and played too long. We were supposed to go upstairs thirty minutes before train leaving time.

The conductor told us that he was going upstairs to the train and we told him we would be there after we played a couple more songs. However, we were having such a good time playing; we let the time slip away from us. I looked at my watch and it was leaving time for the train, so we put up our instruments and started running toward the train. But, we missed the train we were supposed to be on. Fortunately, there was one train, (only one), to leave Chicago, so we could get back home. We apologized to the conductor the next day, but he said it was not a problem because it was a light night. It sure was embarrassing nonetheless.

When we were in our rightful place, we were under the sign that showed where the train stops and the time the train leaves. It was always frustrating to be by these signs, especially when someone came up to ask me where the train stops or what time the 5:40pm train leaves. The people at rush hour resembled a stampede more often than people leaving town.

Chapter Four–Ground Pounder

Again, tired of answering silly questions and putting up with people, I decided to try the freight business. I started out with freight trains coming out of Cicero Yard in Chicago area, going to Savanna, Illinois. I was the head-end brakeman, who followed the engine. That means, as I learned, never letting the engine go by me without getting up on the engine. Otherwise I would be out-of- place (not where I'm supposed to be). We made the trips to the other end of the road stopping occasionally to set off cars and picking up cars going to or beyond our designation.

A crew car would take us from the railroad yard to the boarding house. On one such occasion we had an elderly African-American driving us to boarding house. One of the crewmembers, after an especially bad, sixteen hour trip, without thinking, said, "I think I'll screw a black woman to change my luck." Then thinking who was in the truck, everyone became very, very quiet. After what seemed like an eternity, the driver said, "I don't know, I've been screwing them for 50 years and it hasn't changed my luck yet." This driver turned a tense moment into a very light situation. That was the way to get along rather than take exception to everything anyone says like it is in today's society.

On any run, we went into town to soak up the local culture and dining possibilities. Most times these adventures were like being on vacation, because there was nothing else to do. If you were a drinking man, you would have a few beers or whiskey and then have supper, and then you went to bed to get your rest for your next adventure. Every trip was the same, only the bars or restaurants changed.

While the railroad man was on the road, the spouse had to take care of the household. It was on these trips that I almost lost both of my children. My son was named after my father and me. One day, he became sick and my wife called the pediatrician and he told her, are you ready for this, "Give the child two children's aspirin and call me Monday morning." By the time I arrived at the house, Joe was very sick. I picked him up and where my fingers touched his body, the skin rolled up as if it wasn't attached to him. We decided to take the boy to the doctor and upon seeing our son; he said we had better take him to Des Moines Iowa Medical Center.

When Joe finally got in front of a doctor, there were seven interns around the table. They diagnosed him as having Ritter's Skin Disease. Joe lost every bit of his skin right up to his fingernails and toenails. The doctors said at the time he had a 50/50 chance of living. I'm glad he made it!

Later in my career on another trip, I returned home and my wife said my daughter, Peggy Sue, was sick. Peggy had gotten into one of my shaving bags and took aspirin and chased it with my Mennen after-shave lotion. The doctor told us it was the highest amount of aspirin he had seen in a child that lived. And to think to this day she doesn't like mushrooms.

Being away from my children has been the hardest thing about railroading. I always wanted to be a part of their life, but the railroad kept me from it. If there was one single thing that I regretted in my life, that would be it.

But, I have seen parents that are with their children all the time that are less than a parent than I was. I've been very grateful for my children's look on life and personality, for I think they are tops. My children were taught at a very early age, if they wanted to go out with the adults, they would have to act accordingly. They were always well–mannered because they knew the punishment would come, and they would not enjoy staying at home. They were at their best behavior at restaurants and places where we went where other children could not go because of misbehaving.

When I was working on the freight trains in Chicago, Illinois going to Savanna, Illinois, I worked with a pool shark. I saw him go into bars and clean some those guys out of their cash. He also had a great singing voice and sang in plays at the local theater quite often. I used to bring my guitar on the trips, and we would sing together. He died of cancer at a young age. He was one true gentleman and a nice guy. I learned a lot from him.

One of the freight trains had a car derail at a switch in Waterman, Illinois. The train went one mile with the car on the ground before coming to a crossing. When the derailed car got to the crossing, the car jumped the track and forty-two others followed suit derailing. Forty-three cars were parallel with each other and some stacked three cars high. While looking through the derailment, the track people found two hobos that were killed riding in one of the cars.

Hobos were always riding the trains. Seemed like those people thought the freight cars were made for them to ride. I saw one come out of a coal hopper one day, and although he was Caucasian, he was as black as the ace of spades.

The snow accumulation didn't affect the movement of a main line train. It was curious, though, when we hit a snowdrift, the snow covered the windows so you were blinded momentarily then the snow slipped through the cracks of the door. When the snow hit the heat inside the cab of the engine, the snow turned into a fine mist and hit my face. It was like someone spraying me with a spray bottle. When I had to walk a long way in the snow, it was slow going. I felt like I was moving in slow motion. The muscles in my body would get real tense and tight trying to prevent from falling.

In the wintertime I had to wear so many clothes I looked like I weighed a hundred more pounds more than I actually did. A typical uniform including underwear, long johns, and pants, tee shirt, flannel shirt, insulated overalls, hooded sweatshirt, big heavy coat, and a wool hat. One day my flagman was going to catch our moving train and he missed the grab irons, and fell back into snow on his back.

He was like a turtle lying on his back trying to get up. He had so many clothes on that he couldn't get up, so he had to roll over on his stomach to get on all fours to get up. I laughed a lot over that scene.

While it was good on the road, I had a chance to go on a switcher that was 50 miles from where I lived, and be home every night. Of course, I jumped all over it. The job was in Rochelle, Illinois, where there were a lot of industries. There was Carnation, Swift Inc., a can manufacturing company that made Del Monte cans for their produce. My hours were 7pm to whenever we got off. Usually, that was 6am in the morning. On Saturday mornings, we worked until 11am. That was a long night into day. It made for a short weekend, but the pay was good with all the overtime.

There were fringe benefits of the Rochelle job by getting can goods from damaged cases of food products. I had a station wagon at that time and one night I brought back so much food products in the back that the bumper was almost dragging. I had green beans, corn, hot chocolate, peaches and other stuff that filled up the back of the station wagon. I ended up with a basement full of foodstuffs.

I worked with a bunch of characters on this job that really gave me an education, both in life and railroading. One conductor called "Crazy Coogan" had a theory that if he helped me do the work, we would get done faster and the company would cut off the job. So naturally with him sitting up on the engine sleeping, it took me longer to switch the cars out and do the work. Our pass track was where we switched some 35 to 40 cars for two trains, one eastbound and one westbound and it was about one half of a mile long. We usually put a few cars with hand brakes applied to them into the track to act as a bumping block. Old "Coogan" kicked a car so fast down that track with me on it, that I barely stopped it at the end of the track. I was about one hundred feet before it went over the derail. As cold as it was that night, I was sweating getting that car stopped before it went over the derail and on the ground.

Another guy, Dave Moe, almost got into trouble calling on the company phones long distance to his friends. He used to kid with me, calling me a "hillbilly" and I would call him "Direct Dial Dave." He was a real "Romeo", or so he thought. We had a lot of railroad men that thought they were God's gift to women. One guy named Brandon was in a restaurant hitting on this waitress saying," I sure would like to get into your pants." She said, "One butt hole in my pants is enough." Boy, did he want to crawl under the table and hide from us.

The switching job was a job that I loved because I could see the result of what I was doing. We built the train pick-ups for east and west trains. This was the job where I learned how to switch cars. We pulled all the cars from the industries and normally would have about 30 to 40 cars. We then had to switch them in station order for the trains that came through that night in one track. The cars that went east had to be switched in first with everything else out to the main line. Then we coupled to the train on the main line and switched the west cars into the siding and everything else back out until the west train was built. The cars that were left were transfer cars going to the Chicago and Northwestern Railroad interchange track that was downtown Rochelle, Illinois.

It was on this job that I almost got killed twice. The first time was when ice covered the track on which we were shoving, and the car I was riding on jumped the track. On the adjacent track was a car spotted at Swift Inc. I felt the cars getting closer to my body, so I jumped off the car into the spilled feed waste. The two cars ended up being just 10 inches apart. I may have smelled bad from being in that feed, but at least I was still alive. The other time I almost lost my life was my fault. I was going to release a hand brake from a gondola car from the ground. I looked around the curve of the track to see where the engine was and I thought I had time to do that before they coupled up. I was wrong.

While I was releasing the brake, they coupled up to the other end of the cars causing the gondola to hit me in my chest. The gondola knocked me down on the rail and I saw the wheel of the car coming at me. I rolled over on my side off of the rail as the wheel rolled at me. That scared the mess out of me. My friend, Dave Moe, said I scared the mess out of him also. He said, "I thought I cut you in half you hillbilly S.O.B." That does not stand for sweet, old boy.

A man that was hired about the same time as I was became a victim of a railroad accident. He was coupling the air between two cars when the engine for some reason started moving. He couldn't get out of the way quick enough and the railroad car cut both of his legs off. It doesn't take but a second or a bad decision to be hurt or killed on the railroad.

Somewhere in this timeframe, I bought a motorcycle. It was a 250 Kawasaki, but being a novice, I didn't need a whole lot of power. When I worked in Rockford, Illinois, I rode the bike to work occasionally. There was not much room on the back of the bike, and one day I lost my lunch bucket off the bike somewhere between Rochelle, Illinois and Rockford, Illinois. I didn't have the bike long, and I decided to give it up, so I sold it.

Frank Houston, a conductor, told me once "Riding on a small bike or a moped is like making love to a fat woman, it is fun while you're doing it, but you don't want anyone to see you do it."

The winters were very interesting in Illinois. I remember one Easter in Aurora, Illinois, we had a big snowfall and people were not making snowmen, they made Easter bunnies out of the snow instead. One was around six feet tall with a pink ribbon around the neck of the bunny. At night when we worked, the walking was very tough. The most hazardous was when the snow melted in the daytime to refreeze into ice at night. If it snows a little "dusting" on the ice, the ground was very slick. The muscles in my legs would really cramp up because of being tense and bracing against falling. One night, when I had a situation like this, I busted my butt good time. The ground was very hard also.

We were eighty miles west of Chicago, Illinois and the weather was usually cooler than in the eastern part of the state. One night we had a wind chill factor of thirty degrees below zero. I got off of a boxcar one night, and my leather gloves froze on the side ladder of the car. I had to run alongside the car to get my gloves off the car. It was about that time that I started thinking about going back down to the south to live.

We went to Fayetteville, North Carolina on vacation in the summer of 1972. While in town, I called the railroads all around the city to see if they were hiring any brakemen. The Atlantic Seaboard was not, so I called the Aberdeen & Rockfish. The man there said, "We're the number one railroad" and I said "Really?" He said, "Yes, alphabetically." I always thought that was funny. Anyway, he did tell me that the Southern Railroad was having a hiring session the next day in Greensboro, North Carolina. I felt like I had nothing to lose by going, and maybe I would be hired.

Chapter Five-Railroads and Railroads

The Pennsylvania and New York Central Railroads merged in February of 1968, after years of negotiation and litigation. The new Pennsylvania New York Central Transportation Company acquired the foundering New Haven Railroad in December.

In 1970, the Great Northern; Northern Pacific; Denver Rio Grande; and Chicago, Burlington, and Quincy merged to become the Burlington Northern. The railroad consisted of 25,000 miles of tracks. The railroad became a holding corporation.

There were rumors of extending the 125 mile run from Chicago, Illinois to Savannah, Illinois to go from Chicago, Illinois to St. Paul, Minnesota. It would be a 310 miles run. There would be fewer trains and therefore less crew members. Usually, when we heard of these rumors, they became a reality. The longer runs would mean more pay; because we were paid by the miles ran, rather than an hourly rate. There was a concern among the workforce, because we would be losing jobs and have to go to other jobs, as our seniority allowed us.

True to form, after cutting jobs, I had to go to the Rochelle, Illinois job that was 80 miles west of Chicago, Illinois. There was also a switcher in Oregon, Illinois that I worked sometimes, if I had enough seniority to hold the job. Hoagie was the conductor on that job, so I tried to get on it every chance I had; one because I liked him and two because it was a day job.

Mainly though, I worked six nights a week on the Rochelle job. We switched out Carnation and Del Monte warehouses as well as Swift Company. Swift Company was where they slaughtered cows to be converted into various cuts of meat. Occasionally we would receive damaged cans of food from Carnation and Del Monte that went a long way on our grocery list. The farms around that area supplied the vegetables to Del Monte and they were very fresh.

There was a factory that made the cans that were used in the packing of all these products. On Saturday morning, there was no first shift engine working so we worked 16 hours to complete our switching duties before quitting. My conductor was Coogan. We call him "Crazy Coogan" for good reasons. Someone told me one day at the canning plant he was giving one forklift operator a lot of grief. The operator then said, "I'm nothing but a $5.10 an hour forklift driver and I don't have put up with this!" He then hit "Crazy Coogan" in the head with a ball pin hammer and knocked him out.

I worked 11 hours a day Monday through Thursday and 16 hours on Friday night into Saturday morning. That was a very long day at work. I was so tired Saturday morning, I really couldn't enjoy myself. My favorite hangout was Frankie's'. One Saturday night I brought my guitar and amplifier to the bar and Frankie let me play for a couple of hours entertaining the patrons. I don't think I even bought a beer that night. Someone would request a song and after singing it, they would buy me a beer. At the time, my favorite beer was Pabst Blue Ribbon beer (PBR). I even had groupies that hung around me.

One winter day, I was going home from Oregon, Illinois to Rochelle, Illinois. The ground was covered with snow and I was driving my 1968 Pontiac Lemans. I was passing an 18 wheeler and the two lanes were merging into one. As I was passing the truck, I hit some ice and started sliding. I did a 360 degree turn in the median and came back alongside the big truck, the car straightened out and I punched the gas and just did make it in before my lane was gone. Someone was sure looking after me that day. It was a maneuver I had only seen before on TV at the time.

Michael Swab, with whom I served in the Navy, lived in Chicago, Illinois. We visited him and his wife a lot while I was around Chicago. On one of these visits was the first time I had lox and bagels. It was their traditional breakfast. Bagels, cream, cheese, American cheese, onion, tomato, and smoked salmon. It sure did taste good. I made that meal a lot of times for breakfast myself. We often went camping together and had some very good times.

My family and I made a lot of weekend visits to Hamilton, Illinois where my in-laws lived. Beside the Mississippi River was a scenic route on River Road. It was a very beautiful drive and great scenery. One of rest areas along the river was where John Smith started the Mormon religion before moving to Salt Lake City, Utah. The town was Nauvoo, Illinois. Soon after John Smith was killed in 1844, the Mormons moved to Utah.

There was a restaurant near the yard office in Rochelle, Illinois that we went to a lot of times. What was curious to me was the people would call each other hillbillies. I thought we were closer to the North than the South, but if you look at a map, southern Illinois is about the same latitude as northern North Carolina. The weather in Illinois is rather unpredictable. I had a saying for it, "If you don't like the weather, just wait a minute." The weather could change in a hurry.

The four crew members who went to work in Rochelle, Illinois lived around Aurora, Illinois so we took turns driving, sharing the ride to work. The ride back to Aurora, Illinois took about an hour and a half. One of the crew members had a habit of sleeping while in the car going home, even when driving! Everyone has to stay awake when drove, just in case he went to sleep.

One night at work, it rained hard all night long for 10 hours. I was soaked to the bone. At times when we had a down pour, we just stopped the train and I got under a box car to get out of the rain. When I got off duty, I put on a dry shirt I had in my bag to be somewhat comfortable on the way home.

While driving back to Aurora, Illinois, it was still raining. We came to a spot in the road where the water was running across the road from one field to another. We hit the water at about 55 miles per hour. The Volkswagen station wagon started hydroplaning and we started flipping over and over into the field. The crash broke all windows in the car and we ended up sitting right side up facing the opposite direction.

The experience can be compared to being in a washing machine filled with water and glass. We all went to the hospital to get glass removed from our heads and faces. No other serious injuries. I thought we were very lucky. Since that time I do respect water on the highways a lot more.

During the mid-1970s, seven bankrupt railroads in the Northeast and Midwest were combined into a new company called the

Consolidated Rail Corporation (Conrail). All the railroads seemed to merging into larger railroads forming corporations. At this same time, the Cincinnati and Ohio railroad with the Baltimore and Ohio to form the Chessie System. The same thing was going on in the south. The Atlantic Coastline and the Seaboard Coastline consolidated to become the Seaboard Coastline. Then, these four railroads merged to become the CSX Corp. (M. D. Railroads 2008)

There were starting to be fewer railroads, but through mergers they became larger railroads. On the West coast, the Atkinson, Topeka, and the Santa Fe consolidated with the Southern Pacific railroad to become the Santa Fe Railroad.

Though the diminution and eventual demise of steam was the beginning of the depersonalization of railroading, the process didn't happen overnight. Centralized Traffic Control (CTC) dates back to 1927, when it was introduced on the New York Central, but the 1950s were still rich in train-order railroading, with "flimsies" (orders were generally written or typed on tissue) hooped up to engineers and conductors by agents and operators at thousands of depots and interlocking towers across the country. Though radio was coming in, replacing lantern signals as the preferred communication mode between train and engine crews, it would be years before operating authority could be transmitted over the air. Meanwhile, there were railroaders spread all along the line-and riding the cabooses that trailed every train.

Postwar America through the decade of the 1950s still had the appearance of a railroad country. In 1944, Class 1 railroad mileage totaled 215,493; by 1960 it had actually increased slightly, to 217,552. Over those rails during the decade and a half after the war, a heady mixture of steam and diesels had powered an impressive array of lightweight and heavyweight passenger trains-illustrious all-Pullman flyers, humble locals, and everything in between-and freight trains that ranged from hot "red ball" merchandisers to coal drags, as well as "way freights," serving industries both large and small.

The 40-foot box car was still the emblematic and most common freight car. Stock still moved to slaughterhouse by rail. Many refrigerator cars were still ice-cooled, with huge blocks being wrestled from icing platforms through roof hatches of refrigerator cars. "Loose-car railroading" remained the order of the day, and the unique ability of a train to be combined and recombined at classification yards was held as a primary virtue. If you ordered merchandise, it was still likely to reach you courtesy of the Railway Express Agency, whose green baggage carts stood on the platforms of thousands of depots from coast to coast. So-called L.C.L. shipments ("less than carload lot") shipments were a routine and welcome aspect of the rail freight business.

The Official Guide of the Railways was still a rewardingly hefty tome (Large, heavy book), rich in routes and trains. The modern merger movement lay ahead, so most of the railroad names therein had been familiar ones for generations. Other than the colorful addition of diesels and streamliners, it might seem that little had changed, but forces were already in motion that would soon have serious implications for railroading.

In May of 1949, an ominous milestone was passed. For the first time, airline passenger-miles exceeded those of the Pullman Company. In the 1950s, President Eisenhower signed into law the act creating the Interstate Highway System. America was unmistakably in love with its automobiles, and the federal government decided to make a monumental investment in the roads they would require to dominate the country's surface transportation system.

On March 29, 1957, the New York, Ontario & Western was abandoned. Though this charismatic road has become better loved in death than it ever was in life, the loss of a Class 1 carrier undoubtedly was shocking-a further loss for an industry destined to become increasingly aware of its mortality. (M. D. Railroads 2008)

On March 27, 1960, regularly scheduled passenger steam service in the United States came to an end (except for special excursions like Rio Grande's Silverton Train) when Grand Trunk Western pulled its Northern out of Detroit-Durand local service. Two days later the Canadian Pacific mixed train between Megantic, Quebec, and Brownville Junction, Maine, was dieselized, making moot the question of whether a mixed train was a passenger train.

On May 6, 1960, the Norfolk & Western dieselized, and the twilight of steam faded into night.

Post-war Railroads Timeline

1945: New York, Susquehanna & Western becomes the first Class 1 railroad to embrace diesel technology. Other railroads are quick to follow.

The Chicago, Burlington & Quincy Railroad debuts Silver Dome, the first dome car, on its popular Chicago-Twin Cities Twin Zephyr.

1947: General Motors' four-car, all-dome Train of Tomorrow, a product of its highly competitive Electro-Motive Division, is unveiled at Soldier Field in Chicago on May 28.Alton Railroad becomes part of the Gulf, Mobile & Ohio.

1948: Santa Fe's Chicago-to-Los Angeles Super Chief, successfully inaugurated in 1936 and streamlined in 1937, begins daily service. New York Central fields the all-new Twentieth Century Limited; rival Pennsylvania Railroad counters with a new Broadway Limited.

1949: Burlington, Rio Grande, and Western Pacific launch the Vista-Dome California Zephyr between Chicago and Oakland, California; however, for the first time in history, airline passenger-miles exceed those of the Pullman Company.

1950: President Truman orders U.S. troops to the aid of South Korea.

1953: Norfolk & Western's Roanoke Shops build the last steam locomotive in the United States, an 0-8-0 switcher.

1955: Santa Fe is an early convert to diesel technology, partly due to the scarcity of water on its desert lines.

1959: When a 0-6-0 switcher drops its fires at Camden, New Jersey, the Pennsylvania Railroad is dieselized.

1960: Grand Trunk Western pulls its Northern out of local service in Michigan, putting an end to regularly scheduled passenger steam service in the United States.

Though the 1960s were preeminently the decade in which the privately operated passenger train languished and then died, other significant forces were at work, changing forever the face of railroading. For one thing, 1960 kicked off the modern merger movement, with competitors Erie Railroad and **Delaware,** Lackawanna & Western banding together in October to form Erie Lackawanna. For students of the railroad scene, this amalgamation wasn't that great a shock. Both names survived essentially intact, as DL&W was commonly called "the Lackawanna." Lackawanna's lovely passenger-train paint scheme of maroon, yellow, and gray would adorn all locomotives, but the EL circle-in-a-diamond logo descended directly from the Erie herald.

The next major merger was quite different. In October of 1964, when the Wabash, Nickel Plate Road, and **Pittsburgh & West Virginia** were merged into the Norfolk & Western, their names, colors, and logos vanished down the corridors of time -- as the Virginian's had earlier, after its acquisition by the N&W in 1959.

In 1967, a combination of Seaboard Air Line and Atlantic Coast Line produced Seaboard Coast Line. Then came the merger that characterized the decade -- the disastrous coupling on February 1, 1968, of the **Pennsylvania Railroad and New York Central into Penn Central, with the decrepit New York, New Haven & Hartford** thrown in later (against the wishes of the principal partners). The newly formed railroad's locomotive color scheme was basic black with no adornments. This proved all too appropriate. The new logo, an intertwined "PC," was sometimes called the "mating worms."

More mergers were soon to come, most notably the creation in 1970 of mammoth Burlington Northern from the **Chicago, Burlington & Quincy, Great Northern, Northern Pacific, and Spokane, Portland & Seattle.**

In the 1970s, the process of merging would only accelerate. Illinois Central and Gulf, Mobile & Ohio merged to form Illinois Central Gulf, while the Chessie System was created from the **Baltimore & Ohio, Chesapeake & Ohio, and Western Maryland** lines. In a merger of mergers, Seaboard Coast Line joined with Louisville & Nashville and the Clinchfield Railroad to create Family Lines. In 1980, Chessie and Family Lines would come together to form CSX, in effect, a merger of merged mergers.

The greatest combination of the era wasn't the result of a merger, strictly speaking, but of a government bailout. By the mid-1970s, railroading in the Northeast was in complete disarray. Not only was Penn Central in **bankruptcy**, but so were Erie Lackawanna, Lehigh & Hudson River, and the "anthracite roads" that had once thrived in eastern Pennsylvania's hard-coal country: Lehigh Valley, Reading, and Jersey Central. On April fool's Day in 1976, these railroads (plus a subsidiary, Pennsylvania-Reading Seashore Lines) were consolidated to form Con-rail.

So the operative word in stories of 1960s and '70s railroading is "ended." Passenger trains were discontinued in swelling numbers, and the very concept of passenger transportation by private railroads eventually became obsolete. Great railroad names vanished by the score.

The abandonment of unprofitable branch lines likewise gathered force. What began as a leak in the 1960s would slowly turn into a torrent. Between 1960 and 1980, approximately one fourth of the nation's route miles were abandoned, as branches were pruned and mergers resulted in redundant trackage.

The last Railway Post Office (RPO) car operated on June 30, 1977, between New York City and Washington, D.C. The last non-urban, heavy-duty, mainline, electrified rail service had ended in 1974, when the Milwaukee Road de-energized its track across **Montana and Idaho.**

There were, of course, some new beginnings, and Amtrak was perhaps the most notable - a fragile phoenix of intercity rail service rising from the ashes of the languishing streamliners of the private railroads. Amtrak began operation on May 1, 1971, as a quasi-public corporation that had its genesis in the battles over the **California Zephyr, as well as other discontinuances and downgrading. If a single individual can be called the father of Amtrak, it's probably Anthony Haswell, who in 1968 founded the National Association of Railroad Passengers (NARP), a lobbying and advocacy group that remains a critical force in rail preservation today.**

With Haswell agitating, the press providing coverage, and the government getting into the picture following the 1969 resolution led by **Colorado's Senator Allot, things began to move. The Federal Railroad Administration (FRA) appointed a task force, while the Department of Transportation (DOT), previously opposed to passenger trains, but apparently in a more positive mood under new head John Volpe, on January 18, 1970, released a preliminary plan for what would eventually become Amtrak.**

On May 1, exactly one year before final implementation, the Rail Passenger Service Act of 1970 was introduced, providing for the formation of the National Railroad Passenger Corporation -- or RailPax. A reluctant President Nixon signed the bill into law on October 30.

All railroads then operating long-distance passenger trains (as opposed to commuter services) were eligible to join Amtrak. The cost of admission: roughly half of 1970 losses on passenger service, payable in equipment, cash, or services. The benefits offered in return were enormous, as participating railroads would be free of all future passenger-related losses. Virtually all carriers rushed to join, though a few declined. Rock Island, already financially perilous and less than a decade away from total abandonment, simply couldn't afford the fee, and thus stayed with its surviving pair of short-haul Rockets.

Under the leadership of Graham Claytor (who later served as Amtrak's president during one of the corporation's healthiest eras), Southern Railway opted to run its **New York-New Orleans Southern Crescent**, plus a few lesser trains, on its own. The Rio Grande, not wanting to give Amtrak free rein on its highly scenic, single-track line through the Colorado **Rockies, confused Amtrak's Chicago-to-San Francisco plans by staying out and running its own Denver-to-Salt Lake City Rio Grande Zephyr, using what used to be California Zephyr equipment.**

The rash of mergers had a similar effect on the face of railroading in general, and the demise of the weaker diesel builders led to greater standardization in motive-power as well. Fairbanks-Morse ended production in 1963. Alco threw in the towel in 1969. Baldwin-Lima-Hamilton had built its last locomotive way back in 1956. That left **General Electric** and Electro-Motive Division, the latter still the dominant force in diesel-building. (Brain 2000)

The look and mix of units on the diesel-ready tracks changed radically between 1960 and 1980. Streamlined "cab-unit" diesels were everywhere, wearing the classy, multicolored schemes created in many cases by EMD stylists. "Hood units" -- preeminently Alco's RS3s (RS for "road switcher") and EMD's GP7s and later, GP9s (GP for "general purpose") -- were essentially the same under the skin as the cab units, but with better visibility and easier access to machinery.

The next evolutionary step was to "chop" the short hood for better forward visibility, an innovation of the early 1960s that would typify diesel aesthetics for the next two decades (until the boxy, blunt "safety cabs" of the 1980s). Streamlining and fancy paint schemes seemed superfluous in this hunkered-down era of railroading, characterized by boarded-up depots, abandoned branch lines, and weed-infested rights-of-way. First-generation diesels from all the builders joined **steam trains** in the scrap yards. Utilitarian "chop-nosed" units in a limited number of basic models from EMD and GE were the locomotives appropriate to this era of dramatically lessened expectations. For much of the industry, particularly in the East and Midwest, where the traffic base had eroded badly, survival was virtually all that could be hoped.

But even in these dark days, when the future looked bleak indeed, railroading had begun to reinvent itself. Diesel standardization and perhaps the example of locomotive pooling that occurred naturally in mergers, led to increased power run-throughs from one railroad to another -- an efficient and time-saving practice. Intermodal traffic (trailers and containers on flatcars, otherwise known as TOFC and COFC)-became a significant growth sector, doubling between 1965 and 1980, with the greatest explosion still to come.

Railroads began to exploit other niches with "unit trains" of a single commodity, such as grain or coal. (In 1979, in a rare example of route expansion, Burlington Northern opened its new Powder River Line, tapping rich coalfields in Wyoming.) Centralized traffic control, an idea that was already many decades old, became the norm, along with welded rail.

Railroading is an old-line industry, capital-intensive and labor-intensive, with a thoroughly unionized workforce. Though every gain was won only after a fight, essential work-rules rationalization was begun. The process of eliminating firemen on locomotives, for instance, started as far back as 1964. Crew operating districts, based on divisions that often dated back to railroading's early days (and thus resulted in operating crews receiving a day's pay for a few hour's work) in some cases were revised.

In the final months of 1980, several important events occurred. In December, The Pullman Company was dissolved as a legal entity (though it had ended its staffing of sleeping and parlor cars 11 years earlier), and Northwestern Steel & Wire in Sterling, Illinois, dropped the fires on its refugee fleet of steam locomotives -- engines that this huge scrap yard had chosen to operate, squeezing out a last few useful miles before melting them down for razor blades. This was the last daily, non-tourist steam operation in the United States.

It was less than two months earlier, on October 14, President Jimmy Carter had signed into law the Staggers Rail Act, partially deregulating the railroads. This event was significant. It was the go-ahead for the railroad industry, however dramatically redefined and slimmed down, to "highball it" once again.

1960s and 1970s Railroads Timeline

1960: The Erie Railroad merges with competitor Delaware, Lackawanna & Western to form the Erie Lackawanna Railroad.

1963: After a U.S. ship is attacked, Congress endorses the Tonkin Gulf Resolution, authorizing U.S. involvement in the Vietnam.New England's troubled Rutland Railroad is abandoned. Sections of the line soon reopen as the Vermont Central Railroad and the Green Mountain Railroad.

1965: New York City's Pennsylvania Station is razed in December, sparking a landmarks preservation movement that continues to this day.

1968: Pennsylvania Railroad and New York Central merge to form Penn Central.

1969: The Pullman Company's staffing of sleeping cars ends as of January 1.

1970: In this frenzied time of mergers, Chicago, Burlington & Quincy; Great Northern; Northern Pacific; and Spokane, Portland & Seattle combine, forming Burlington Northern. The Interstate Commerce Commission reluctantly allows the demise of the legendary California Zephyr.

1971: Amtrak takes over most passenger-train operations in the United States. Auto-Train begins service in December, carrying automobiles and their occupants between Lorton, Virginia, and Sanford, Florida.

1973: A fleet of French-built Turbo liners are delivered to the United States, marking fledgling Amtrak's first new equipment acquisition.

1976: Conrail begins operation as a result of the consolidation of Penn Central; Erie-Lackawanna; Reading; Lehigh Valley; Jersey Central; Lehigh & Hudson River; and Pennsylvania-Reading Seashore lines on April 1.

1979: The first double-deck Superliner cars enter service for Amtrak.

Railroads of the modern era jumped at the chance to become bigger and more efficient. For years, the largest of the railroads were referred to as the Super Seven. Today, that number has been whittled down even further. The stage is set for a day in the near future when there will be two major rail systems in the West; three in the East; a few regional railroads running secondary rail lines unwanted by their larger cousins; and hundreds of short lines taking over smaller branch lines.

Through a series of mergers, several super-railroads have been created. These giant railroads take several forms. Some are the creation of a marriage of equals-such as Chessie System and Family Lines, or Norfolk & Western and Southern, or the combination of Burlington Northern and Santa Fe in the mid-1990s. (1990s 2008)

The Burlington Northern-Santa Fe merger created the nation's largest railroad, with almost 30,000 miles of track. Even before the merger, Burlington was the nation's biggest coal hauler. Thanks to the demand for low sulfur coal from Wyoming's Powder River Basin, BN hauls more coal for utilities than any other railroad in the nation. Santa Fe's specialty was the high-speed piggyback train, toting truck trailers and containers across the nation. From Chicago to Los Angeles, Santa Fe's silver and red "war bonnet" paint scheme led some of the country's fastest TOFC (Trailer on Flat Car) runs.

Taking a different approach, Union Pacific has grown by purchasing railroads. Over the last 15 years, the UP has acquired the Western Pacific, Missouri Pacific, Missouri-Kansas-Texas, and Chicago & North Western, Southern Pacific, and Denver & Rio Grande Western lines, creating a blanket across the west and the Midwest.

At the end of 1995, Union Pacific sought to bring Southern Pacific-itself a combination of the SP and Rio Grande-under its control, to counterbalance the BN-Santa Fe combination. That made the UP the nation's largest railroad with slightly more than 30,000 miles. The move came more than a decade after an early 1980s attempt to merge the Santa Fe and Southern Pacific. That deal went awry when the I.C.C. failed to give its approval.

Ironically, the dream of a true transcontinental railroad remains just that-a dream. In all of the mergers of recent years, none has dared unsettle the balance of trading partners on either side of the Mississippi River. That is likely to change some time in the twenty-first century. Industry experts point out that it is only a matter of time before mergers between the remaining East Coast and West Coast railroads take place. The U.S. railroad map may eventually show three, or perhaps two, major rail systems crisscrossing the mighty Mississippi.

The super-railroads of today are a reflection of other U.S. mergers and mega-companies of the modern era. As railroad companies merge, they are able to concentrate more authority in fewer managers, dictating orders across a wider area.

As is often the case, unproductive parallel rail lines and antiquated equipment typically become surplus after a merger. In the case of many mergers, these surplus lines quickly become fodder for regional railroads, short lines, and railroad museums. Regionals and short lines often succeeded where the super-railroads failed, due to lower costs and less restrictive work rules.

Several of these lines have found a niche. Montana Rail Link, for example, began operating Burlington Northern former Northern Pacific line, no longer needed because of plenty of capacity on the paralleling Great Northern line. Today, Montana Rail Link is a healthy company, with almost 1,000 miles of track and almost 100 diesel locomotives moving paper, forest products, grain, and other commodities. Other companies, such as RailTex, of San Antonio, Texas, operate several short lines of less than 100 miles each from one central headquarters.

The efficiency of the super-railroad is a stunning example of American business at work. Railroad stocks have outperformed the overall U.S. stock market since 1991. At the same time, freight rates have fallen in inflation-adjusted dollars. The industry has begun to take back traffic it lost to trucks and barges in the years since World War II. Freight shipments reached record levels for seven years in a row through 1994. The railroads' share of intercity freight rose to 39.2 percent in 1994, up from 38.1 percent in 1993 and 37.5 percent in 1992.

Even before they adopted a new paint scheme on their locomotives, the Burlington Northern and Santa Fe went to work immediately after their merger in 1995 to streamline their operations and launch an intermodal train service between California and the Southeast. The new service bypassed the Burlington, whose lines were packed with coal trains bound from the Powder River Basin in Wyoming to utility plants in the South, in favor of the higher-speed Santa Fe lines across the West. The improvement sliced 24 hours from the scheduled run between San Bernardino, California, and Atlanta, Georgia.

Two of the most exciting technological developments have come with the introduction of double-stack containers and RoadRailers. Double-stacks rely on a flatcar with a sunken floor that allows two intermodal containers to rest one atop the other, doubling the capacity of a flatcar. Southern Pacific was the first major railroad to build these cars, in conjunction with ACF Industries.

Double-stack containers often arrive by ship, and then continue their journey by train, with final delivery by truck. Double-stack trains have necessitated the rebuilding of many routes on the nation's mainline railroads to accommodate these ultra-high loads. The clearance of bridges and tunnels were raised in Pennsylvania in a multimillion-dollar project to get double-stack service to the port of Philadelphia. In Virginia, Norfolk Southern eliminated or renovated several tunnels on its hilly line into West Virginia to allow double-stacks to pass between Chicago and the port of Norfolk.

Double-stacks have won back much of the profitable perishable-goods business for the railroads. Replacing the traditional refrigerated boxcar is the 40-foot-long double-stack container, powered by a generator with an automatic backup in case the main generator fails. With double-stack trains running between Seattle and New York in only five days, everything from Alaskan king crab to photographic film can be shipped in temperature-controlled boxes.

In 1977, according to data from the Association of American Railroads, railroads carried only 0.2 percent of produce shipments. After deregulation, perishable traffic jumped to 15 percent. A container, which can make several trips in one month's time, easily outperforms refrigerated boxcars, which by comparison average only one trip a month.

On other railroads, particularly Norfolk Southern, RoadRailers are the current rage. Basically a truck trailer that can ride the rails or the highways, these lightweight, versatile containers operate in dedicated trains of 100 cars or more, moving everything from beer to cat litter. Detachable rail wheels make them easy to put on the tracks, while retractable wheels make them easy to put on the road. Both have meant big gains in productivity.

The railroads redesigned everything. They built new hopper cars to carry the nation's coal for electric power plants, switching to lighter and more durable aluminum designs, and they revamped the traditional wood-hauling car to make it easier to load and unload. They even replaced the wooden tie and spike with concrete ties and metal clamps.

Communications technology has also revolutionized some aspects of railroading. Throughout the industry's history, train crews have left their terminals with a manifest of pre-assigned duties, pickups, and set-offs. On the Union Pacific, the railroad started using a direct-link computer system between the crews and the marketing department. That means reporting immediately when cars are distributed or collected. It also means flexibility in sending service orders to a train on the road.

In Roanoke, Virginia, Norfolk Southern has a giant freight yard resembling a big remote-controlled model railroad. Computers set the brakes on the cars being sorted in the railroad's hump yard. They also align the switches. Operators sitting in a strategically positioned tower even manipulate the pace of locomotives shoving cars through the yard.

New freight-car wheel designs have reduced the number of accidents resulting from wheel failure by 80 percent. By changing the shape of the wheel and subjecting the steel to heat treatment, professional engineers have literally reinvented the railroad wheel.

Advances in technology have had their price, however. Railroad employment has been particularly hard hit. Today's railroads haul more freight than they did at the beginning of the 1980s, but they do so with 40 percent fewer employees. (1990s 2008)

From 1979 through 1992, the output per hour in the railroad industry rose 8.1 percent, according to the Bureau of Labor Statistics. That made U.S. railroads the most productive in the world. Railroad productivity increased 157 percent from 1983 to 1992.

In addition, many sweeping labor agreements have changed the face of the industry. A 1982 agreement reduced the number of crew members on a freight train from four or five to two or three. Early 1980s agreements also spelled the end for the caboose-from then on, the conductor would ride in the locomotive with the rest of the crew.

After a strike in 1991, the Brotherhood of Locomotive Engineers won a wage hike that hasn't kept up with the rate of inflation. The union also gave up some health benefits and agreed to work more hours before getting overtime pay. As a result, an Amtrak passenger train that once required four crews to complete the trip from Washington, D.C., to Atlanta, Georgia, now operates with only two.

Such changes resulted in drastic reductions in employment at the nation's major railroads, whose work forces dipped from 475,000 at the dawn of the new era to some 191,000 at the end of 1993. The trend is expected to continue, as technology and computers make railroading safer and more efficient with fewer workers. Someday, through-trains may run by radio signal from remote-controlled dispatching centers, trimming the crew to a single person.

The railroad industry is taking a second look at virtually everything it does to squeeze more profit and efficiency from its operations. Freight cars once tracked by human clerks as trains entered yards now respond to radio signals that can beam their codes directly into a computer.

Amtrak, the nation's federally subsidized passenger railroad, has likewise begun moving toward a new era. With its budget tied directly to federal subsidies, however, it has weathered a difficult era in which money to buy new equipment has been tight.

The purchase of millions of dollars worth of new Super-liner passenger cars at the beginning of the 1990s and a newly designed car known as the View liner spelled the end for the streamlined passenger-car fleet of the 1950s. The first of some 140 new Super liners resulted in entirely new versions of popular Amtrak trains such as the Cardinal and the Capitol Limited.

Steps to improve Amtrak service between Washington, D.C., and New York City have seen travel times trimmed, with steps being taken to increase speeds from the 120-miles-per-hour range into the 140s. Congress allocated millions of dollars to increase speeds through computer-aided dispatching, higher-speed track, and new electric locomotives.

Perhaps the most encouraging signs that Amtrak was ready to make a leap forward came in 1993. Amtrak tested the Swedish X2000, German ICE, and Spanish Talgo-all advanced trains. These new trains operate with special devices that allow them to travel at higher speeds on curves. Computer-controlled devices actually tilt the X2000 to give it the ability to flash through curves at speeds much higher than normal. Such trains are envisioned as the next step toward faster service between cities. In the extreme Northeast, they're seen as the key toward extending high-speed service from New York City into highly congested New England.

If successful, high-speed rail lines will spread from the Northeast into other sections of the nation. Modern trains will glide along banked turns and fenced-off right-of-ways to move passengers from city to city in record time.

The University of Texas Center of Electro mechanics, for example, has been awarded $2.9 million to develop an advanced passenger locomotive that can accelerate faster. If super-railroads, big technological changes, and sweeping labor reforms were unexpected at the beginning of the 1980s, the next few years could be even more surprising.

Just as the steel railroad car replaced the wooden one, and the diesel replaced the steam engine, it's reasonable to expect even more change from the major railroads in the years to come.

More and more powerful locomotives aided by computers that track everything from the adhesion of the wheels on the rail to the performance of the motors will be pulling trains in the near future. Dedicated trains in which each rail car is powered, thus providing for smooth starting, stopping, and operation, is one possibility.

Intermodal traffic, which has grown more than 60 percent in the last decade, is expected to jump another 60 percent in the next few years. Fast intermodal trains roll across the Colorado high plains on the Santa Fe line as Q-trains and on the nearby Union Pacific line as Z-trains or "Zippers."

Railroads will become better utilized thanks to satellite tracking and computerized signaling and safety devices. As the nation continues to wrestle with environmental problems, the railroads will continue to be an important resource, moving the same amount of freight with only a tenth of the pollution.

The first reviews on deregulation seem to be positive. A shippers group called CURE (Customers United for Rail Equity) sought to partially re-regulate the industry beginning in 1986, but made little progress. In vindication of the 1980 Staggers Act, the federal government in late 1995 dismantled the Interstate Commerce Commission. Debate focused on which remaining federal agencies would assume the I.C.C.'s duties to hear rate disputes and merger cases. The future of the railroad as a free-market industry looked secure.

Throughout their more than 170-year history, American railroads have reflected the development of this diverse and changing country. They grew up with the nation in the 1830s and spearheaded the drive west. They turned ever more complex and, by the turn of the century, became the province of wealthy speculators. They went to war twice in this century. And facing the new world after World War II, they struggled with old ways of doing things.

Today, they're obsessed with technology and productivity, as our society demands newer, faster, and better ways of doing things. In that sense, the railroad is a mirror of American culture. Never before has it been involved in so many new ways of doing what it does best-carrying freight and passengers. As many American industries are busy trying to "re-engineer" their companies, the railroads are well into almost one generation's worth of experimentation and change.

Need proof? Watch what happens south of Seattle late on a springtime afternoon. At a mainline crossing where both Union Pacific and Burlington Northern are within feet of each other, the gates flash and come down. The headlight of a southbound Burlington Northern train appears. Quickly, its two diesels and string of double-stack containers whizz by. The sound of the engines is a deep roar, like a baritone clearing his throat. The tracks sing as the cars pass beneath them. In the distance, a small beacon, the conductor of the twenty-first century, flashes red, sending out an electronic greeting.

Or watch on a sunny Sunday afternoon as a giant CSX coal train rolls through Marietta, Georgia, on its way from a Kentucky coal mine to a Florida power plant. Two AC-powered engines roll the 13,000-ton train south almost effortlessly. Gone forever are the laboring steamers, stopping regularly for water and coal.

Gone, too, are many of the doubts about railroading's future. The industry is headed full throttle toward the twenty-first century, and it's not looking back.

Chapter Six-Back to Me

I arrived at 400 S. Elm Street in Greensboro, North Carolina in 1972 where the Division headquarters were located right at 8 o'clock. The railroad has always been very strict about things happening on time, even if they start late, they want you to be on time. After taking the usual tests and filling out numerous applications, I received several forms for me to take to three different doctors. Two of these forms had to be completed by doctors the next day, so I had to spend the night in Greensboro, North Carolina, and go to the doctors' office the next morning.

I spent the night at the Coliseum Motel that night, because it was the closest hotel to Elm Street. The next day I went to the hospital to have more tests and x-rays taken. I started out with 20/20 vision, no broken bones, good hearing, good attitude, and the picture of health. Southern even had to run a police check on everyone. Nowadays, if you are convicted of a felon, you will not be hired or if working, you will be dismissed from service. After being in Greensboro, North Carolina for the better part of the day, I went back to Fayetteville, North Carolina. The Trainmaster said the company would notify me at home in Illinois if they hired me. Wow, what a prodding. There was no bone unturned or no brain cell unpicked. I always figured the railroad wanted you in good physical condition, so they alone could ruin it.

After we had been back to Illinois for about a month, the Southern Railroad called me and told me I could come on down and start my training. I asked the Trainmaster if I had the job and he said, "No, you can start your training." This was going to be taking a chance to uproot the family and move back to North Carolina and start all over. Weighing everything, we decided to go south.

Well, just like the Beverly Hillbillies, we loaded up our rented truck with all of our belongings and the family car and headed south. We arrived in Salisbury, North Carolina in July 1972. We checked into the first hotel we came to off of Interstate 85. With the heat on the trip and the length of travel, our parakeet died that was riding in the backseat of the 1968 Pontiac. We buried the parakeet on the grounds behind the motel.

We looked in the newspaper for a place to rent. Being very hot, when we found a duplex that simply advertised "air-conditioned $125 a month", we rented that apartment. The duplex was just off of Dunn's Mountain Road and Walton Road. Later, I found out Philip Walton, who worked on the railroad as well, was my neighbor.

I got my schedule for my training period from the Trainmaster and was set to go to work. Just up the road from me lived Phil Walton and in another house lived his Dad. The road was obviously named after them. Phil also worked for the Southern Railroad Co. and I had to train with him on the Lexington switcher. That was the first job that I trained on for the Southern railroad. The crew met at a bank parking lot across from the entrance of Spencer Yard and drove to Lexington, North Carolina where the engine was kept.

Spencer Yard stretched from Spencer, North Carolina on the north end to Salisbury four miles south where it ended at 11th Street. The yard and town were named after Southern Railroad's first President Samuel Spencer. The town had a lot of people that worked in the rail yards. Spencer Shops were located there at one time in the early 1900s, a facility that repaired cars and locomotives at the yard before being closed down and moved to other towns.

Chapter Seven- The Diesel

Sometime in the forties the diesel-electric engines were introduced. They were more powerful and lots easier to operate than the steam engines, at least in my opinion. To hear the old railroad men talk, the steam engines carried 100 cars at 90 miles an hour every day. There are a lot of people who do not know how the diesel engines works. I'll try to explain it to you as simply as I can. First you start with a diesel engine that is connected to a crankshaft to the main generator.

The main generator is connected to power cables to the traction motors. The traction motors have gears at the ends of them geared to the wheels. Thus, the diesel engine turns the crankshaft that supplies the electricity from the main generator to the traction motors that turn the wheels. Clear as mud huh?

One big difference between a diesel engine and a gas engine is in the injection process. Most car engines use port injection or a carburetor. A port injection system injects fuel just prior to the intake stroke (outside the cylinder). A carburetor mixes air and fuel long before the air enters the cylinder. In a car engine, therefore, all of the fuel is loaded into the cylinder during the intake stroke and then compressed. The compression of the fuel/air mixture limits the compression ratio of the engine -- if it compresses the air too much, the fuel/air mixture spontaneously ignites and causes knocking. Because it causes excessive heat, knocking can damage the engine. Diesel engines use direct fuel injection - the diesel fuel is injected directly into the cylinder.

The injector on a diesel engine is its most complex component and has been the subject of a great deal of experimentation -- in any particular engine, it may be located in a variety of places. The injector has to be able to withstand the temperature and pressure inside the cylinder and still deliver the fuel in a fine mist. Getting the mist circulated in the cylinder so that it is evenly distributed is also a problem, so some diesel engines employ special induction valves, pre-combustion chambers or other devices to swirl the air in the combustion chamber or otherwise improve the ignition and combustion process.

Some diesel engines contain a glow plug. When a diesel engine is cold, the compression process may not raise the air to a high enough temperature to ignite the fuel. The glow plug is an electrically heated wire (think of the hot wires you see in a toaster) that heats the combustion chambers and raises the air temperature when the engine is cold so that the engine can start.

All functions in a modern engine are controlled by the ECM communicating with an elaborate set of sensors measuring everything from R.P.M. to engine coolant and oil temperatures and even engine position (i.e. T.D.C.). Glow plugs are rarely used today on larger engines. The ECM senses ambient air temperature and retards the timing of the engine in cold weather so the injector sprays the fuel at a later time. The air in the cylinder is compressed more, creating more heat, which aids in starting. Smaller engines and engines that do not have such advanced computer control use glow plugs to solve the cold-starting problem. Of course, mechanics aren't the only difference between diesel engines and gasoline engines. There's also the issue of the fuel itself.

Chapter Eight- The Southern

The pioneering South Carolina Canal and Rail Road Company, Southern Railway's earliest predecessor line and one of the first railroads in the United States, was chartered in December 1827 and ran the nation's first regularly scheduled steam powered passenger train – the wood-burning Best Friend of Charleston – over a six mile section out of Charleston, South Carolina, on December 25, 1830. (The Baltimore and Ohio Railroad ran regular passenger service later that year.) By 1833, its 136-mile line to Hamburg, South Carolina, was the longest in the world.

As railroad fever struck other Southern states, networks gradually spread across the South and even across the Allegheny Mountains. Charleston, South Carolina, and Memphis, Tennessee, were linked by 1857, although rail expansion halted with the start of the Civil War. The Richmond and York River Railroad, which operated from the Pamunkey River at West Point, Virginia to Richmond, Virginia, was a major focus of George McClellan's 1862 Peninsular Campaign, which culminated in the Seven Days Battles and devastated the tiny rail link. The Richmond and Danville Railroad was the Confederacy's last link to Richmond, and transported Jefferson Davis and his cabinet to Danville, Virginia just before the fall of Richmond in April, 1865.

Known as the "First Railroad War," the Civil War left the South's railroads and economy devastated. Most of the railroads, however, were repaired, reorganized and operated again. In the area along the Ohio River and Mississippi River, construction of new railroads continued throughout Reconstruction. The Richmond and Danville

System expanded throughout the South during this period, but was overextended, and came upon financial troubles in 1893, when control was lost to financier J.P. Morgan, who reorganized it as the Southern Railway System.

Southern Railway, as it came into existence in 1894, was a combination of the Richmond and Danville system and the East Tennessee, Virginia and Georgia Railroad. The company owned two-thirds of the 4,400 miles of line it operated, and the rest was held through leases, operating agreements and stock ownership. Southern also controlled the Alabama Great Southern and the Georgia Southern and Florida, which operated separately, and it had an interest in the Central of Georgia.

Southern Railway's first president, Samuel Spencer, drew more lines into Southern Railway's core system. During his 12-year term, the railway built new shops at Knoxville, Tennessee, and Atlanta, Georgia and purchased more equipment. He moved the company's service away from an agricultural dependence on tobacco and cotton and centered its efforts on diversifying traffic and industrial development. Sadly, Spencer was killed in a train wreck in 1906.

By the time the line from Meridian, Mississippi, to New Orleans, Louisiana was acquired in 1916 under Southern Railway's president Fairfax Harrison, the railroad had attained the 8,000-mile, 13-state system that marked its territorial limits for almost half a century. The Central of Georgia became part of the system in 1963, and the former Norfolk Southern Railway was acquired in 1974.

Southern and its predecessors were responsible for many firsts in the industry. Starting in 1833, its predecessor, the South Carolina Canal and Rail Road, was the first to carry passengers, U.S. troops and mail on steam-powered trains, and it was the first to operate at night. The Southern Railway was notably the first Class I railroad in the United States to completely convert to diesel motive power. On June 17, 1953, the railroad's last steam-powered freight train arrived behind 2-8-2 locomotive No. 6330 in Chattanooga, Tennessee.

From dieselization and shop and yard modernization, to computers and the development of special cars and the unit coal train, Southern often was on the cutting edge of change, earning the company its catch phrase, "Southern Gives a Green Light to Innovation." This was the logo painted on the Southern Railway box cars; along with "Southern Serves the South."

Every hood unit locomotive Southern owned was ordered with a high hood and operated long hood forward for crew safety in case of accidents with vehicles. From the first GP7 to the last GP50, they came with this option until the tradition stopped with the SD50. This in effect, would require no extra switching of the locomotives to put a short nose forward. I always preferred to see where I was going, rather than to plan for a collision with other trains or vehicles.

In the early 1960s, a popular steam locomotive excursion program was instituted under the presidency of W. Graham Claytor, Jr. The steam program survived the merger which formed the new Norfolk Southern Railway in 1982, but was finally discontinued in 1994. I remember one of my friends had a set off of cars in Lynchburg, Virginia. He did not ride the rear of the cars like he was supposed to, and the cars ran into the excursion train cars damaging them pretty bad. It was soon thereafter, that Southern Railway discontinued the steam excursions.

In 1974, the Southern merged old Norfolk & Southern Railway into a company subsidiary, the Carolina & Northwestern. It was at this time we stopped terminating our trains in Selma, North Carolina and started terminating the trains in Raleigh, North Carolina in the old NS yard.

On June 1, 1982, after receiving ICC sanction, the Norfolk & Western and the Southern merged into the newly formed holding company, Norfolk Southern Corporation. Under the agreement, each share of NW common stock was converted into one share of Norfolk Southern common stock, and each share of Southern common stock was converted into 1.9 shares of Norfolk Southern common stock. The result was that Norfolk Southern Corporation attained 100 percent voting control of NW and 93.9 percent voting control of the Southern.

Chapter Nine- Spencer Yard

Spencer was thriving town in the early 1900's. The railroad was big and the town was growing. In 1903 there was a mail train (Old 97) that became famous through a song that ran on the Eastern division from Monroe, Virginia to Spencer North Carolina. The song was very popular and made the train famous. The story goes on to say that an inexperienced engineer not familiar with the road was running the train and lost control of it, and crashed near the Dan River in Danville, Virginia.

The story goes on to say his nickname was "Steve" (Broady). Years later, as I was Secretary/Treasurer of Division 375 of the Brotherhood of Locomotive Engineers, I found an index card with his vital information on it. I can now say that his name was G.A. Broady born July 5, 1877. He became an engineer 7/27/1902 and retired 12/31/1952. It shows on the card that he died April 5, 1956. Finding this card with "Steve's" information on it sure did give me goose bumps.

In those days, there were several passenger trains and many freight trains. The passenger train was called the Southern Crescent. Passenger service was preferred service and the older men in seniority were on those jobs. Anyway, I didn't have to qualify on the passenger trains, but I did have to work on the jobs that I would be working. After training on various assignments on the division, the Trainmaster "marked me up" on the "extra board".

"Marking up" is a term meaning placing your name on the active working list. The "extra board" is a term for the list of names of people who are called to work when the "regular assigned" person is "off", meaning off the list of working people. This is confusing to lots of people because if you "mark up" when you are working, then why wouldn't you "mark down" if you don't want to work? Then if you "mark off" from working, why wouldn't you "mark on" to go back to work? That is the reason the railroad language is a different language than any other. Anyone you talk to in railroad language, unless they worked for the railroad, they will look at you as if you have two heads.

I guess at the back of this book, I should put in all the definitions of all the slang or phrases of railroading so people will know what I am talking about. There are so many, plus the fact that on other districts or railroads, they may have another terminology all to themselves. How the plot does thicken!

When I went on the Lexington switcher with Phil Walton, he told me not to tell anyone about my prior railroad experience because they would get jealous about my knowing more about the job than someone who had just started railroading. I thought that was good information that Phil gave me and it was true, as I found out.

The Conductor on the Lexington switcher was Sam Gordon. He mumbled when he talked so bad, it was hard to understand what he said, making it double hard to learn the job. Sam walked with a limp, because the rumor I heard was that a railroad car was rolling away and when he tried to stop it, he put his foot under the wheel to stop it. The wheel cut part of his foot off. Sometimes, the first impulse you have could be the wrong choice.

Each assignment (job) had four crewmembers: Conductor, Engineer, Flagman and Brakeman. The Conductor is in charge of the train and the switching of cars. He takes care of the waybills (bill of lading for each car), and instructs the Flagman and the Brakeman in their duties. The Engineer is jointly responsible for the train and operates the locomotive engines. The Flagman is usually the field (railroad yard) man that tends to the cars in the various tracks. The head-end brakeman is usually the youngest member of the crew that throws the switches, changing the engine or cars from one track to the other.

If the job was an industry switcher, we needed all of these people to help, for it was enough work for everyone. On some of the road jobs we needed all of crew for there were a lot of work on them also. Sometimes, the crews were called for a train that was a "hot shot". The hardest thing the crew had to do get up on the train at the "initial terminal" and get off at the "final terminal." Of course, the Engineer of the train had to work equally on all of trains. After all, who's going to move the engine, if not the Engineer?

The general public usually does not know one person's job or "position" on the train from the other. Even in the movie "Emperor of the North", Hollywood said the "Engineer of the freight train was keeping hobos off of the train", when it was actually the Conductor doing it. I think it would be hard for an Engineer to "drive" a steam engine on the front of a train and keep hobos off of the train at the rear. In fact the newspapers normally have no idea. One paper reported that the Conductor was blowing the whistle of the train involved in a train-car collision. I'm sorry, but all the controls for operating the engine are usually on the Engineer's side of the engine. Unless, of course, the conductor was sitting in the engineers lap! I hope not.

Okay, back to the story, I'll explain more about all the job responsibilities later. One of the assignments that I had to work as a trainee was the second shift Reidsville switcher. The Conductor of the job was Harold Jones. He and I became close friends. Later on, when I lived in Greensboro, North Carolina, Harold and I went to NCAA basketball tournament games together at the Greensboro Coliseum. We watched Duke in the first round. I had brought a pint of whiskey to liven up the soda. When we finished it in the first game and we still had another game to go, Harold said, "Next time you'll have to bring more whiskey."

Also on the job was a newly marked up brakeman named Allen Stone. We nicknamed him "Pebbles" and "Stony". Having prior railroad experience, Harold stated that the job was working as well as if he had two brakemen on the job.

This was only because I had worked as a brakeman for two and one half years on Burlington Northern. "Pebbles" was a nice guy, but he had such a high–pitched voice that after listening to him for about five minutes, your ears would hurt. Anyway, I called the trainmaster to see if I could be "marked up" because I already knew how to do this work and he said, "You're supposed to be watching, not working." I thought that was quite dumb, because the more you watch, the better you get at watching. However, after thirty days, I was marked up on the brakeman's extra list.

I started out on the Spencer extra board that supplied brakemen to the vacancies to the yard at Spencer and all the road jobs. At that time, there were two separate boards, one for the road, and one for the yard. I liked the road better because it suited me better than just going back and forth on the yard all day. First, you go in one direction and then the next, one direction then the next. I felt at the time that would drive me crazy, if I had to do that all day. But that was the engineer that was going back and forth, not the brakeman.

When I finally got marked up, I was forced as the youngest marked-up man to an outlying job (Burlington Switcher) in Burlington, North Carolina. One of the brakemen on the job was Tom Barber. He had also been forced to this job when he became marked-up as the youngest man. He was glad to see me, because he asked the Call Office to relieve him with me, so he could go back home. That is exactly what they did, because of my lack of seniority. The regular conductor of the job was Freeman Yow. He had been "fired" for rule "G" before and according was a reformed drunk (AA).

Being "fired" I found out was being suspended from service without pay. Rule "G" was the abusing alcohol or drugs rule. In those days, it was not uncommon to have people drink on the job. It seemed to come with the territory. There were many stories of crew members having to be hauled up and put on the train because they were still drunk when they came to work. That may have been one of the reasons there were so many railroaders killed in those days. It was not all the reasons though. I remember when we were called to relieve a train's crew that had only gone ten miles, Monroe, Virginia to Lynchburg, Virginia.

We found out that the conductor had stepped off the caboose at around midnight to check the numbers of the cars ahead of caboose. The only bad thing about that was that the cab was in the middle of a bridge with no walkway. He fell off the bridge about 40 feet to his death. On one other occasion, a brakeman walked out in the track to watch a train go by and he walked right in the path of the train and got killed.

One of the rules was to inspect the passing trains for any defects. The only mistake he made was to walk off the cab on the mainline side instead of going on the off side of the caboose where there was no train. I had just weeks before that, played the guitar with him. Just like I have said earlier, the slightest error in judgment could cost you your life.

The railroad really used me and I worked most every day. The brakeman job was interesting enough, but the officials on the Southern were such hard noses and they seemed to be proud of the fact that they were so asinine. They were at their best when they could hide in the bushes and catch someone doing anything against the rules, so they could go up to them and reprimand them. They did this even if, when they were in the same job before being an officer of the company, they did the same thing. They were a total different person when they became an officer of the company.

If any of our fellow workers saw a Trainmaster hiding in the bushes somewhere, he/she would alert the others by saying, "There's a snake in the grass at Lexington". That would alert them to be on their best behavior. One of Trainmasters came up to me one day and said, "Joe, what's this I hear you've been telling everyone I'm a Son-of-a-Bitch?" I said, "It wasn't me Mr. Terry, I don't know how they found out!"

I had to give Phil Walton credit because of what he said about people being jealous of my prior railroad experience, for they sure were. It was like they thought I was out to get their job for knowing what I did. Oh well, if they had to be jealous, so be it. I wasn't going to worry about it. At this time, in my braking days, there were only two places to take freight trains. One was 165 miles from Spencer Yard to Monroe, Virginia. The other was to go to Selma, North Carolina (159 miles).

The main line crews going to Monroe, Virginia always called the East line crews "cheese-eaters". They were called that because the crewmembers would eat either cheese crackers or hoop cheese going down the line to Selma, North Carolina. There was a dormitory at the end of the trip waiting for the train crew. Both had kitchens in them so if you brought any food with you, you were able to cook for yourself. That way, you would have something to eat. If you didn't bring anything with you, you didn't have anything to eat. The nearest store was one mile away and the railroad did not provide any transportation for you to get something to eat to survive on.

In the dormitory, there was a refrigerator provided. The food you put in there for yourself was not always there when you came back for it. Some people, who didn't bring any food, would just help themselves to whatever they wanted in the refrigerator, if they became hungry. Some of the guys were really good cooks and could survive very well. The regular crews would plan their meals the trip before and would not be short on food when they began to cook. Each crewmember would bring a certain item or items and when they arrived at the dormitory at Selma, North Carolina they had all the makings for a dinner. It was like a picnic, except more elaborate.

In Monroe, Virginia, however, you were ten miles from town. Some of the regular crews had a car at the dormitory and would drive into town to eat. They would charge you fifty cents to a dollar to ride along with them. That wasn't a bad price, all things considered. The only other choice you had was to eat junk food out of the machines to survive. What I did was bring the food to cook, so I was not at the mercy of someone else and I knew what I was eating.

The downside of that was if I did not have my food in a locked container, some butt face would go into the refrigerator for my food, as if someone put the food in the refrigerator for them. On one occasion, I made some coffee and I left the kitchen for a few minutes to pack my bag for the trip home. When I came back downstairs one of those butts came out of the kitchen with a cup of my coffee in his cup. I called out that he was a S.O.B (not sweet old boy), but I doubted that he heard me or that he even cared, for that was the normal for the butt-holes to feed off of other people.

I was on a work train as a flagman around Selma, North Carolina for about eleven days. It was not the custom for the railroad to provide a hotel for you while you were away from home, but this time they did. The four crew members shared adjoining rooms at a Holiday Inn. Each room had two double beds in them. The conductor and I shared one room, while the engineer and brakeman shared the other.

I had a 1970 Volkswagen at that time, and I drove it down to Selma so we would have transportation to go eat. The conductor went out one night and hooked up with a couple of women and he spent the night at their house. He called me the next morning to go get him so he could go to work. While we were getting ready for work, we opened the door between our rooms. When the engineer looked into our room, he saw one made up bed and one messed up bed. He kept glancing from one bed to the other, and then he finally said, "Good God, did you boys sleep together last night?" I have had a lot of fun telling that story over the years.

Chapter Ten –Becoming an Engineer

Everyone always asks me, "How do you become an Engineer?" At that time, the railroad promoted the firemen to engineers when they needed more engineers. However at this time, there were no firemen to promote, so they asked the trainmen to submit a letter of interest to the Superintendent in becoming an engineer. Being that I had only a year of seniority as a brakeman, I decided to go for it. I made up my mind to become an engineer sooner than some of the "older guys" in seniority, and as a result, I went to engineer school ahead of them and jumped around them in seniority as a fireman, then to an engineer.

When I entered into engine service, I had to become a fireman first and was placed on a passenger train. I was on the passenger train to both learn the road and learn about the duties as an engineer. I was placed on the Southern Crescent passenger train with engineer Sam Sharpe. I eventually bought the house in Spencer, North Carolina that Sam Sharpe's father lived in before he died. The heating system was a huge pot bellied stove in the basement. He burned pieces of railroad ties in the potbellied stove for heat. The smoke from creosol in the crossties that burned in the stove, darkened all the walls on the upper floors, and we had to paint the whole house to get the smudge off.

On the other side of the assignment of the passenger train was engineer Joe Beale. I worked with him sometimes also. We stayed on the passenger train until it was our turn to go to engineer school in Birmingham, Alabama. I went to school there in October of 1973.

The railroad provided a hotel room for you while you were in school and provided you with three meals a day also. While I was in

Birmingham, I looked up a friend, James Roberts, I served with in the U.S. Navy and we went out on the town a couple of nights. It was good to see him again, although it had only been ten years since I had seen him. After a month in school, I came back home to start the "on the job training" for six months to learn the road and assignments in our area.

Along with jobs (assignments) or "runs" I learned as a brakeman, I had to learn more to be an engineer. I had to learn jobs in Salisbury, Spencer, Lexington, Thomasville, High Point, Greensboro, Reidsville, Burlington, Durham, Raleigh, Selma, and Goldsboro, North Carolina. Also, I had to learn the jobs in Danville, Altavista, Hurt, Monroe and Lynchburg, Virginia. Some of the towns had multiple jobs, both day shift and night shift, and I had to learn them all in case you were called for them one day off the extra board.

There were flagging rules we had to learn for reducing the speed of the trains. These were rules I had to abide by to slow or stop the following trains, so they would not run into the rear of our train. The rules included the use of flares and torpedoes. Torpedoes were a small explosive device that we strapped to the rail intended to alert the engineer of a following train to slow down and look for the rear of the train ahead of him.

These were placed on the rail around one to one and half miles before the train was to be stopped for any delay such a setting off or picking up cars or switching cars. Any time a train was stopped on dark territory, that is tracks with no signals, we had to make the arrangements for the protection of the rear of the train by following trains, so they would not run into the rear of the train.

The torpedoes would make a small explosion or noise loud enough for the train crew to hear over the roar of the train or engine. When the engineer heard this, he had to reduce the speed of the train, so he could stop at a flagman with a fusee or flare, protecting the rear of the train. If the train left after working, we still had to slow down and be looking out for a train or other obstruction, for we would not know what we were going to encounter.

It could be a "rule check", where an officer of the company would be checking to see if you were complying with the rules. They could be the person holding the fusee, to see if you were slowing down and be able to stop. If you went by him, without stopping, you would be pulled "out of service" for not controlling your train properly.

The Volkswagen that I had was bright orange. When I was helping Tom Graham build yet another house in Salisbury, North, Carolina, I arrived in my "Bug". The driveway was really steep and Tom told me, "Chock my truck with that orange rock." After that day, we named the car "The Orange Rock." While building the house, we were running out of 16 penny nails, so Tom sent me to the hardware store to get some more. I didn't know what type to get, so I what I bought was common nails. I did not know that Tom preferred the coated nails, because they sink into wood a lot easier. When Tom and I started hammering the nails that I had purchased, they were ricocheting everywhere, because they were not coated and were not seating very well. Tom said in his slow country drawl, "Junior, next time you get nails, don't buy the pretty, shiny ones."

Chapter Eleven-Running the Road

Some of the runs were in the daytime, but there were more runs at night. During the training, it was best to operate trains in the daytime so you could learn how the lay of the land was and how the tracks went uphill or downhill. Learning the road in daylight helped you know how to operate the train at night. I was able to know where the curves and hills were. As simple as it is to know that you increased speed going up the hill and decrease speed going down the hill, you can see drivers in their cars on the highway that do not understand that theory.

When I was hauling 12,000 tons of freight, I had to go after the speed quickly in the bottoms to avoid losing speed too fast to avoid stalling on the hill. Once lost, the speed is hard to gain, especially if you are moving a lot of tonnage. When I started a train with a lot of freight cars, I had to start out moving the throttle real slow until the slack of all the rail cars are out and the rear of the train is moving. If I used too much throttle too quickly, I could tear the train up. This meaning that you could break a knuckle or a drawbar that is holding each rail car together.

If this happened, the brakeman or conductor had to walk back to this separation, and somehow get a 50 pound knuckle to replace the one that was broken. The engineer would throw a knuckle on the ground and pull the car with the broken knuckle up to that point, so the brakeman would not have to carry the knuckle all the way back to the separation. Once replaced, the train was coupled together again and on its way. This would normally take from 30 minutes to 90 minutes to complete the job. If the train separated in single track, all other trains waiting to use the single track would have to just sit and wait.

Young engineers that "mishandled the train" broke knuckles, or if you became relaxed in operating the train, could cause the slack to break the knuckles. The training that you went through, taught you how to be a good train handler. The crew member on the caboose would tell you when the slack of the train was either in or out, so you could adjust the throttle as necessary. I tried to operate the train to keep the slack either in or out, because slack in the train was usually the cause of broken knuckles. If you controlled the slack of the train, you had less of a chance to have the train come apart with broken knuckles.

On the territory that the engineers operated the train, the road foreman, which is the officer of the company over engineers and firemen, had special instructions for handling trains at some of the bad spots where engineers broke a lot of knuckles. The instructions even told you what throttle notch to be in (0-8) to handle slack at any particular location. Even if you went through these areas without tearing the train up, they would discipline us for not following the stated procedures.

Although most of the engineers on the Danville District allowed the engineer trainees to operate a train, there were some that didn't trust anyone to operate their train. One engineer, Ray Eller, did not allow me to operate his train all night long, until we started up White Oak Mountain. It is 10 miles uphill and all you had to do was to put the throttle in number eight (Maximum-numbered one through eight) and kick back and relax, for you could do nothing else. After that trip, I decided I would no longer need any training from that engineer.

It took me six months to complete all the assignments that were listed on my training sheet. On every assignment, the engineer had to sign his signature on my training paper that I had completed that assignment. At this time, I felt confident enough to qualify as an engineer. The Road Foreman of Engines had to set up a trip with the General Road Foreman of Engines to make a trip with me to see how I handled the train. This qualifying trip was usually on one of our "hotshots" that was only on duty five hours or less.

The General Road Foreman of Engines was usually a nice person. Seems to me like, the higher the person is in standing on the management ladder, the less BS goes with them. Anyway, I operated the train in accordance with the rules and regulations and the General

Road Foreman of Engines qualified me to be marked up as an engineer. I became an engineer on May 14, 1974. I was placed on the extra list. The next day, I was called to go to work on train 342 going to Monroe, Virginia, which usually worked all night.

Trains going North and East were even-numbered trains and trains going South and West were odd-number trains. In 1974, trains either went to Monroe, Virginia or Selma, North Carolina. The two types of trains going to Monroe, Virginia were "Hot Shots" or "Slop Freight" (Also called dead freight; trains that made a lot of setoffs and/or pickups.) These trains had to pick up cars in all the smaller towns between Spencer, North Carolina and Monroe, Virginia; that the local freight or switcher jobs pulled from industries and plants.

The Hot Shots were called that because of no stops or no delays and made the 165 mile run in four hours or less. These trains were either "Piggyback" trains or trains with cars of high revenue. Those trains went into Potomac Yard (Pot Yard), in Washington, DC. If they made it there before midnight, the train cars wouldn't have to be charged with another day per diem for being on Southern Railway's tracks. The Hot Shots came out of Atlanta, Georgia or Columbia, South Carolina. The engineer would operate the train only on his district. The train would come into the start of another district, stop, change crews, and be off and running again.

Sometimes, the train would just slow down real slow and the outbound crew would get up while the train was still moving. This was call swapping crews "on the fly". The hot shots normally changed crews on the main line so there would be minimum delay.

Normally, crews would have to go to the roundhouse to get their engines. Now, they call it the Diesel Shop, for it is no longer round. I would go on duty at the engineer's washroom where I had to check on the current bulletins listed in the books on the table. Listed in the bulletins, could be tracks out of service speed restrictions on the whole district that I was supposed to memorize, and other information.

Once I got to the roundhouse, I would check to see what engines we would be using that day. The head end brakeman would usually go on duty at the washroom with the engineer, while the conductor and flagman would go on duty at the yard office. The yard office was where all the company clerks were, as well as the yardmasters, trainmasters, and the superintendent of the terminal had his office.

In the old days, the clerks had to walk each track and write down the car numbers for each car on paper or switch lists. You can tell this was before computers. The yard was basically flat and we had to do all the switching of cars the old fashioned way. The engineer would give the cars a little speed and the brakeman would "pull the pin" to uncouple the car to let it roll free into the track you wanted it to go. We would have to have some cars in that track with hand brakes applied to them or otherwise, the car would roll out of the other end of track, which is not a good thing.

Each track held cars going to the same destination. For example, if we had cars going to ten different locations coupled to the engine, we would switch them to different tracks. Then, we would get another group of cars (a cut) and switch them out until the whole train you were working on was switched out (all cars in their proper places).

Another switch engine on the other end of the track made sure the cars were all together and placed track of cars to build outbound trains. The track was placed under blue flag protection for the car inspectors to inspect and couple the air hoses together between the cars. After the brake test was complete, the train was released to the yardmaster, and then crew caller had to arrange for a crew to be called to take the train to its destination.

This was also coordinated with the diesel shop to arrange the engines to pull the train. Sometimes, this worked out well and everything fell into place as planned. However, the reason for the title of this book is because, that was rare when everything worked together.

For example, maybe they didn't call the crews correctly, the engines were not there when the crew was, or the train wasn't ready. Then there could be other trains or train movements in your way so you couldn't get to your train. Too many variables and "Murphy's Law" was always present. I have been on trains for several hours and couldn't get the train ready to leave the yard.

They would just call another crew that had more "time to work." By Federal Railroad Administration (FRA) rules, we could only work for twelve hours and then we had to be relieved by another crew, no matter where we were.

If everything went well in the yard and we were ready to leave, we could still sit in the yard until the main line dispatcher was ready for you to go out on the main line. Other trains could be out on the main line and there would be no room for our train – again, too many variables.

The dispatcher's office was at Elm Street in Greensboro, North Carolina. The dispatchers controlled the switches and signals at their office on the main line for 333 miles (Washington, DC to Salisbury, North Carolina). Some of the dispatchers I knew very well and we were friends. Sometimes the dispatchers would ride a train so they could learn the territory where they were dispatching trains.

On one such trip, a dispatcher was riding with me and it was a rather warm day. We were on a train in the siding at McCleansville, NC (8 miles from Greensboro, NC) waiting for another train. The dispatcher knew the conductor on that train and asked him on the radio if he had anything cold to drink? When the caboose slowed to meet our engines, the dispatcher was shocked when the conductor handed him a cold Old Milwaukee beer. After the shock was over, the dispatcher started laughing.

When the train was ready to go, we had to get permission to leave the yard from the yardmaster. The yardmaster checked with the main line dispatcher to see if he was ready for us to leave. If there was not any conflicting traffic, we were told to leave the yard.

Starting and stopping trains were the most difficult. When starting the train, I would start the throttle very slowly to move one car at a time. Typically a train consisted of three or four engines, about a hundred to one hundred fifty cars, and a caboose. Moving the throttle slow to move one car at a time, would prevent the last car from starting too fast (jerking it.) I could hear trains starting too fast, because the slack of the cars came out too quickly and the cars would be jumping and rumbling making an awful racket.

When entering and leaving yards, I had to go at a speed that would permit me to stop in one-half of my sight distance. The reason was just in case, another train or engine was on the same track; I would be able to stop before hitting the other train. All the speed restrictions required the engineer to stop short of any obstruction of other trains. Naturally, the faster the train goes, the harder it is to stop and more distance it goes before stopping. Everyone thinks a train can just stop when we want to stop, but that is not the case.

Trains were superior to other trains by class and direction. First class trains were superior to second and third class trains and second class trains were superior and had the right of way over third class and extra trains. If trains were operating by the timetable, second and third class trains had to clear the main line for the first class trains to operate on the main line. Extra trains had to display white flags or white lights on the front of their train to show they were not a regular train (first, second or third class trains.) Passenger trains were considered as first class trains.

All the crew members of the train were required to have watches compared with each other and not be off by a couple of seconds per month. In steam engine days, inferior trains had to be in a siding, clear of the main line, by five minutes of the time a regular train was supposed to be at that station. It was not uncommon to have train collisions because crews pushed the limits of their time by not clearing the main lines.

At the beginning of each run, the engineer and conductor received train orders from the dispatcher. A clearance card was with the train orders clearing the train with authority to operate in dark territory. In those orders stated the sidings each train had to clear the main line to let other trains run. On the rail line from Greensboro, North Carolina to Selma, North Carolina, there was no signal system.

Before electric switches were installed at Greensboro, crews had to throw the switches by hand adjacent to the dispatcher's office to line the train for Selma, North Carolina. After lining up the switches on the main line, the brakeman received the train orders from the dispatcher on the second floor of the division office building. I then pulled the train through the turnout so that the conductor on the caboose could talk me down to a stop to line the switches back for the main line and get his train orders.

The train orders were made in triplicate, one for engineer, conductor, and copy on file for the dispatcher. The train orders were so thin that we called them onion skin paper. No train could run in dark territory unless they had train orders.

Chapter Twelve-Life on the Road

Other than the main line trains, there were also local freights. They could be call road switchers, turn a rounds, or local freight trains. These trains switched cars in the industries, mills and factories that had rail service. These jobs had regular engineers on them, but if they were off sick or on vacation, their position was filled by the extra board in Spencer.

The most undesirable away from home vacancies filled by the Spencer extra board were Altavista, Virginia and Goldsboro, North Carolina. Altavista, Virginia was 130 miles from Spencer and Goldsboro, North Carolina was 180 miles. At that time, the company didn't pay for any lodging for us, so I was on my own to find a place to stay, so I didn't have to drive back and forth to home. After a week, these positions were filled by the youngest (in seniority) engineer on the extra board. This was called being forced to job. I sure didn't go that far away from home willingly.

I served my time at the away from home terminals like other low seniority engineers. Some of the places I slept would surprise most people. There were times I had to sleep on a caboose to get a night's rest. Of course, there were no showers on there, so you would clean and shave the best you could in bathrooms. This sure wasn't the Holiday Inn.

Being away from home long periods of time was just another part of being a railroad person. Then, in addition, to being on the extra board, I never knew where I would be going next or when I would be going out on a job. We had a saying on the extra board, "It's either feast or famine." That meaning, I could work most of every day and make a lot of money, or you could be at home for a long time and make little or no money.

The extra board engineers usually made more money than regular assigned engineers because of working all the time. There was a variety of jobs that made the job interesting. All the work trains or extra board assignments went to the extra board. The work trains were cars of company material like railroad ties or sections of rail to be unloaded. When call for a work train, I had no idea if it was to be for one day or two weeks. It is very difficult to pack an overnight bag for two weeks of clothing and food. We never knew when the next meal time would be or where it would be.

For that reason, I had to take with me some drinks, can goods, and snacks to survive until I could get to a place for a real meal. Often, the bag was so heavy; the straps were stressed to the breaking point. Most of the train crews carry two bags with them, one for clothes and railroad materials and one for food and survival. Oftentimes, I felt like a pack mule for all the things I had to carry.

I preferred the road jobs rather than the yard jobs, switching cars and making up trains was a 24 hour job and you never finish. On the road jobs it seemed like I had a sense of accomplishment after the run for completing a successful trip and delivering the train to a destination. I stayed on the road extra board for a few years until my seniority allowed to me to be on a regular job.

Along with an accurate watch that I had to have inspected annually, I had to have a current timetable for the division and a rule book in my possession at all times. The timetable was a list of all the trains that ran on our district with the times they were due to arrive at each station.

There were eleven regular jobs going to Monroe, VA and five regular jobs going to Selma, NC. These jobs had regular assigned trains to operate and have an off day built in the assignments. I would work 4 days then be off one day, then repeat the cycle. The trains operated everyday so the off day was formatted so you did not work every day. I still had to answer the phone receiving my call to go to work, but at least I knew about what time it was going to be.

I had to live by the phone when I was on the extra board. It felt more like a prison at my own home not knowing when a call could come to go to work. If I had to leave the house, I would have to call the call office for updates on the trains coming.

Living by the phone was the worst part of being a railroad man. I had to get a beeper so, if I left the house for anything, I wouldn't miss my call for work. It really felt like I had ankle braces on so I couldn't leave the house. When I got up in the morning, I would call the call office to see what job I stood for. If they said the train would be called about 2pm to 4pm, then I would try to rest or take a nap to be prepared to work 12 hours without being tired. Then when I called back about 1pm or 2pm, they would say the train is going to be later, like 6pm to 8pm. By this time I couldn't rest for I was ready to go. When the call office finally called me for the train, I was tired again.

There were other times when I called the call office and the clerk told me there were no vacancies or any jobs open. I would leave the house to go fishing or something. The call office would call me for some Phantom Train that dropped out of the sky. I would have to hustle back home to go to work. For instance, one day I called up the call office and they told me no jobs were in sight to be filled. Before I could get to the lake, my beeper went off and I had to go back home and prepare to work.

Working on a regular job was a whole lot better than the extra board. At least you were able to plan some occasion later on in the month if you were off duty that day.

I finally won a bid on an East run and I became a regular engineer on a Spencer to Raleigh job. I was on a regular assigned crew for the first time as an engineer. The conductor on the crew was James Winstead. The flagman was Joe Tucker. This was truly a party crew and with enough experience to make a fine running crew. When we were going to Selma, North Carolina, we would plan our meals in advance for the next trip. Each crew member would bring something for the meal. One man would bring the meat, another would bring a vegetable or two, and another would bring the salad, and so forth. When we arrived at the dormitory, we would cook the meal and eat together. After dining, we would clean up the kitchen.

When the company moved the assignment to Raleigh, North Carolina, we stayed at the Holiday Inn on North Boulevard and had to go out to restaurants to eat. Eating out in the restaurants costs a lot more money for expenses on a trip. However, there were several different food establishments within walking distance of the hotel. Of course, before we went to eat, we would have to go to the liquor store (ABC).

Each of the guys would have a different choice at the liquor store, so when we set up the bar in the hotel room, it truly looked like a bar.

After we registered at the hotel, we went to our rooms, cleaned up, and went to the designated bar-room. We would share stories of the day's events as well as other trips that were memorable in one way or another. Although we would not like to talk about railroading, the conversation usually came back to it.

Sometimes, I would take my guitar on the trip with me and I would entertain the crew with songs and picking. If there were other guitar pickers on the job, we would play together. We would drink two to three hours, then go out to eat. After eating, we would go back to the hotel and go to sleep. If we were lucky, we would get about five or six hours sleep. After we had been off duty eight hours, they could call us to work.

There was a lot of the remodeling to do in the 13 room house that I bought. It seemed like when I had free time from the railroad, my time was spent doing carpenter work and painting. We remodeled kitchen and painted all the rooms. The bathrooms had the old bath tubs with feet on them.

While I was doing the carpenter work, I was always going to the lumber store for two by fours, nails, and paint. At this store, was where I met Bill Haithcock. I also found out Bill liked playing the guitar, also. He came over to our house, and we play the guitars together. Sometimes, when I was off, I would go to lunch with Bill. We went to a restaurant where they had a pinball machine. After lunch, we would play the pinball machine until it was time for him to go back to work. We could play for a long time on just one quarter. Bill, at one time, rented a room from me, so we were able to play our guitars together for hours on end. My children were in elementary school then, so Bill and I worked up a routine and performed for the whole school.

Bill played softball a lot after work, and came home very tired. We were talking one night and he asked me how the diesel-electric locomotive worked. He was listening to me as I explained how the diesel engine supply power to the main generator, then the power went to the traction motors, and so forth. While I was talking, I noticed that Bill had fallen asleep, so I stopped talking. After a brief time, Bill looked up and asked, "Was I through?" He fell asleep and didn't know who was talking.

While I was on an East run, I hit my first vehicle with a train. I was coming into Greensboro from Raleigh on Train No. 83 at 20 mph. The crossing was equipped with flashing red lights and cross bucks. The car with three people in the car tried to beat me to the crossing. They didn't make it. The engine hit the left rear quarter panel and I put the train into emergency. No one was killed in the collision, but it did total the car.

On one trip coming back from Raleigh, North Carolina, we were coming out of Mebane, North Carolina going downhill toward Haw River. I saw a car on the tracks, but I didn't see anyone around the car. We nailed the car right in the passenger side. Needless to say, we totaled the car. We figured out, someone just wanted to get rid of their car and have the railroad pay for it. People actually did that, and the railroad would pay these people just to stay out of court. The ironic thing about this incident was that years later, someone established a junk yard there, and I can't help but think that I contributed to their inventory.

On another trip on an East Run, I was going uphill out of Burlington, North Carolina at night, when I saw what I thought was a box on the rail. When I got closer though, I saw it was a person sitting on the rail. When I sounded the whistle for him to move out of the way, all he did was fall forward into the gauge of the track. We were only going 20 MPH, I but could not stop before killing him. As soon as I hit him, I smelled alcohol and blood. That was my first fatality with the train.

It seemed that when people wanted to drink, they would go on the railroad tracks to consume their beverage. The police would not bother them for they were on private property, even though it was the railroad's property. The railroad did not have enough railroad police to keep trespassers off of the hundreds of miles of track. There were numerous fatalities that occurred when people got drunk and passed out on the track. Many did not even know what hit them.

Another time, I was going through Durham, NC and another car tried to beat me to the crossing. I hit the car on the passenger side at 20 mph. Even at this slow speed, it still took almost a half of a mile to stop the train. The rookie policeman that came to investigate this collision asked me for "my driver's license and registration card." Of course, we do not have registration cards like automobiles for the locomotives. It seemed to me that people always blamed the train crew for not stopping to avoid hitting people. They just don't know that it takes a long time for a train to stop. Sometimes, up to a mile or longer.

Still again, on another trip through Durham, we came around a curve and there was a paving machine sitting on the tracks paving an approach to a crossing. I sounded the whistle over and over again for the operator to get out of the way. When he leaped off of the equipment, I knew it was not going to move on its own, so I put the train into emergency braking.

Unlike on television programs, the wheels do not slide or go in reverse making sparks. This was one of the times I was glad the long end was forward on the locomotive. The locomotive pushed the grade-all down the tracks and the equipment caught on fire. The fire started coming into the window of the locomotive. The other two crewmembers and I immediately left the engine compartment and leaped off to safety. The heat from the fire melted a good part of the inside of the engine, destroying all of our personal belongings.

Anytime an employee is injured on the railroad, he settles with the claim agent on an agreed settlement for their lost-time injuries from the job they were on. If they cannot agree on a dollar amount, the employee will hire an attorney to work for him. Most of the attorneys come from a blue collar city with people who had sympathy for the working man. Such was the case in the collision with the grade-all. I had to go to Birmingham, Alabama as a company witness.

Both of the employees suing the company, which were hurt in the collision, were friends of mine and I was put into a situation against them and their lawyer. Their lawyer had a simple plan. He wanted me to get on the stand and admit that I was speeding, and that is the reason we were in that collision and the railroad workers were hurt. Well, I could see how that would help him out a lot, but that would put all the responsibility on me. I figured out who the lawyers were going to use as a scapegoat, so I told him what he could kiss.

After being in court for a week, the jury decided against the company and the employee won the lawsuit. One of my friends came up to me and said I could have helped his lawyer out a little bit. He wanted me to lie for him, so he could get more money from the lawsuit. Oh well, tough! He sure didn't care about me taking the fall for all of that. After settling for a certain amount of money for those two employees, I asked the claim agent to reimburse me for my lost of my personal bag.

Would you believe, he said he couldn't do that after going to bat for the company in that lawsuit. He screwed me out of $50. I received nothing from that collision! They got the gold mine and I got the shaft!

The lawyers sure did take me out to some nice places to eat while in Birmingham. I think the main idea was to keep me away from the employees' lawyers and talking to them. Aside from the court case, I had a good time in Birmingham.

I can see how the employees would not like dealing with the claim agent. After all, he is paid by the railroad company. I twisted my ankle when I was a brakeman. I was walking through the weeds to go to the engine, and a kudzu vine caught my foot. I went head over heels. I missed three weeks of work because of a sprained ankle. The company doctor released me to go back to work after nine days. Heck, I still couldn't walk without limping, yet.

Anyway, after I returned to work, I went to the claim agent to settle up for my lost time. I had to barter with him over how much I should settle for. When I signed the waiver to go back to work and releasing the company for my injury, the claim agent said "Now, if your leg falls off, it won't matter." I felt like smacking him upside his head!

The Norfolk Southern Railway, in 1970, had rail lines going from Raleigh, North Carolina to Chocowinity, North Carolina; Raleigh, North Carolina to Fayetteville, North Carolina; and Raleigh, North Carolina to Charlotte, North Carolina. There were rumors going around at that time that Southern Railway was going to merge with the old Norfolk Southern. The rumors became true in 1974. We stopped going to Selma, North Carolina and started terminating our trains in Raleigh, North Carolina.

We no longer had to stay in a dormitory for we were staying in the Holiday Inn on Capitol Blvd. in Raleigh, North Carolina. I actually felt like a real person, unlike the conditions we had to live in the dormitories. The rail yard in Raleigh, North Carolina was much smaller than the one in Selma, North Carolina. Also, the rail yard was laid out on a hill, where the rail yard in Selma, North Carolina was flat. This made a difference in controlling the train, for I was always going uphill or downhill.

Going into Raleigh, North Carolina on a train was a real test of the engineers' ability to operate their train. At the top of the hill by the state fairgrounds, we went down a three mile grade though the middle of North Carolina State University. When we passed the state prison, we had to go around a sharp curve at ten mph, and then down another grade for two miles before reaching the yard.

Just around the ten mph curve, about the distance of one half of a block, was an absolute signal. The signal could be displaying a "stop" signal. I made arrangements to stop at the signal, because the amount of air brakes I used to slow down for the curve, I couldn't release them fast enough to proceed without stopping. Several engineers have been suspended from service for running by that particular stop signal.

The main problem with that signal was the interlocking was controlled by the CSX dispatcher in Jacksonville, Florida. There are two main line tracks from Cary, North Carolina to Raleigh, North Carolina. One track was controlled by CSX and the other track controlled by the Southern Railway. It was hard enough to contact our own dispatcher, but then to be able to contact another one. That signal was to allow a train to utilize the crossover from the mainline to get on the lead going to the rail yard in Raleigh.

When a train was going though Mooresville, North Carolina (between Durham, North Carolina and Cary, North Carolina), the engineer would call Boylan Tower (The operator at Raleigh) by radio to let him know we were coming to Cary, North Carolina. The operator would then call the CSX dispatcher for him to lineup the electric switches and give our route a green light.

The placement of the signal at Cary, North Carolina was another bad location. After coming up a four mile grade, we had to go over two road crossings and around a curve to see the signal. The signal would not come into view until you were about 300 feet from it. If we had a stop signal, the train would be blocking two main crossings in Cary, North Carolina. These signals sure did seem to me to be placed in awkward locations. We had to be ready to stop at those signals, even though the dispatcher would tell us "I am ready for you." Later on the company did put them in a position we could see them, before reaching the first crossing.

After getting on to double track, we would call the yardmaster in Raleigh to let him know we were coming his way. The yardmaster would instruct us on the tracks we were to place the train. Most of the time, we pulled the rear of the train into one track, and then doubled the head of the train into another track. To further complicate the move, there was a derail at the end of each track in the yard. A derail is a piece of iron designed to derail a train or rail cars so they will not run into the side of another train on another track.

When we arrived at the North end of Raleigh yard, we had to cross the CSX mainline again. There was a control box at the end of the yard where we had to activate a button to receive a signal for our movement. If there were no conflicting traffic, the signal would turn green for us to proceed. The Raleigh yard was small, so if we came in with 100 or so rail cars, we would have to double or triple over 60 or so cars.

The procedure for this move would go something like this. First, we would stop the rear of the train in the clear in the first track, usually the longest track. After applying the air brakes on the train, the brakeman would apply hand brakes on several of the rail cars to be left in the track. Secondly, the brakeman would uncouple the train portion to be doubled over and the engineer would pull forward. After stopping over the switch, the brakeman would line the switches for the next track for the remaining rail cars. The brakeman would communicate to the engineer that the switches were lined and to start backing up. The flagman of the train would tell the engineer how far to come back into the track. When we filled that track up with cars, I would apply the air brakes and again the brakeman would secure that portion of the train. We would repeat as necessary until the train was secured in all of the tracks.

When we were left with just the engines, we would ask the yardmaster the route he wanted us to go to the diesel shop. All of the shop tracks had derails in them, also. After stopping in the diesel shop, we applied the hand brakes on the locomotives. At this point, we could gather up our personal belongings and get off of the train. When our taxi had arrived, we loaded up in it and went to the hotel. All of this was normally accomplished in two or three hours. Sometimes, it was longer and sometimes it was shorter in time.

The crews were called in order as they arrived in Raleigh as when they were called in Spencer, North Carolina. There were no regular times for trains to be called, so we waited in the hotel until we were called for a train to go home. The wait could be as little as eight hours and as long as 40 hours or more. After we were off duty at the away from home terminal or 16 hours, we received detention time. That is an hourly rate of pay until we were called for a train to go home, up to eight hours pay.

I was in the hotel room all night one trip and the crew caller did not call me for a train. However, he did call the other crew members. The conductor, flagman, and brakeman received their calls, got into the taxi, and went to the yard office. As they were getting their train orders, engine numbers, and the tracks the train was in, the flagman said to the conductor, "Do you think we should tell them we don't have a driver (engineer)?" So, they all loaded up into a taxi and went back to the hotel and waited for the call office to call me to go to work. I found out then that they could leave any of the other crew members, but they could not leave the engineer.

Along with places to eat, there were a lot of night clubs near the Holiday Inn, as well as a nightclub in the hotel itself. A lot of the guys had girlfriends and Raleigh, North Carolina and the road between Spencer, North Carolina and Raleigh became known as the (Alimony Road). We were young, we worked hard and we played at the same speed. I was working with good friends and they were also very good railroad workers.

In the summer time, we always made sure we had plenty of the ice and water. At the beginning of each trip, at that time, we used galvanized igloo water coolers and paper cups. Some guys to put their soda cans in the water cooler, which would cause etching. Not to mention, putting their hands in the water to get their drinks after they were cold. It was not very sanitary. I would make ice and water for the crew, but I would take my own personal cooler with my own drinks in it, or get another cooler for drinks only. On hot days and long days working, we could drink all of the water. Years later, Southern Railway bought cheap bottled water and Styrofoam coolers for the train crews to use. The coolers were so fragile that they broke easily and leaked all over the floor of the cab of the engine. It didn't take long before the company had to get more durable 64 quart capacity plastic coolers that were large and bulky.

When we met other trains at sidings, we had to watch the crews for mischief. Often, in the summertime, our fellow workers would throw ice water on us as we met. I did not want to get wet, so I did not play these games. One time, I was going down the hill at Raleigh, North Carolina, and I had the engine door opened to get some air. A fellow worker was taunting the other crew as we were meeting the train going uphill. One of the crew members on the other train through water at my guy and he ducked in behind the wall of the engine. Because I could not move from the engineers' seat, the water hit me in the face at about 30 miles an hour. The force of the water knocked off my hat and safety glasses. Later, I found out who did it and I told him he'd better not ever do that to me again, or I would stomp his butt. He didn't do it again either. Too many people get hurt from that sort of horse play.

There were rumors going around that the company was going to build a new rail yard to replace Spencer Yard. It was not long after those rumors; the company started grading for a new yard in Linwood, North Carolina. The land stretched from Linwood to the Yadkin River. The yard was to be built parallel to the two main line tracks. The land was so wet and swampy, thousands of tons of gravel had to be hauled in from Danville, Virginia and other gravel pits.

I was separated from my first wife at that time and lived in a mobile home a little while. Then, I moved into an apartment on Lee Street in Salisbury, North Carolina. To say I moved out of the big house in Spencer with a lot of stuff would be erroneous. I had everything I owned with me, including my guitar, in my Volkswagen and I had plenty of room. I was a victim of "alimony Road", for I was one of the guys that had a girlfriend in Raleigh, North Carolina. I met her at Valentine's, the nightclub inside the Holiday Inn. The interesting part about this is she was born and raised around Stedman, North Carolina, where I went to high school. We lived around eight miles from one another, but never knew each other. We would recall a lot of places around Fayetteville, North Carolina we both knew about.

With the new yard being built, it was just a matter of time before the move of all operations from Spencer, North Carolina to Linwood, North Carolina. When the company shut down Spencer Yard, I planned to move to Raleigh, North Carolina. The Goldsboro local went to work in Durham, North Carolina and I figured I would go to that job, because it was only 30 miles from Raleigh. The company would post a bulletin abolishing all the jobs in Spencer seven days before establishing the jobs in Linwood, North Carolina.

My friends knew of my intention to move to Raleigh, North Carolina when they abolished the jobs for the move to the new yard. On one of my trips coming into Spencer, North Carolina, as I was reaching the south end of the yard, my conductor met me with some news. He said, "Joe, they have advertised the jobs to reassign them for your move." I told James, "It has been nice working with you, but I am moving to Raleigh." He said that he understood and we said our goodbyes. I called my girlfriend, Dixie (yes, that was her real name), and asked her if I could move in with her. She said yes, so I made the move in my 1970 orange Volkswagen and moved to Raleigh.

Chapter Thirteen-Life on the Locals

I made my seniority move to the Goldsboro local that went on duty in Durham, North Carolina. There were two Goldsboro locals; Train 64 going from to Durham, North Carolina to Goldsboro, North Carolina, and Train 63 going from Goldsboro, North Carolina to Durham, North Carolina. The switches for these industries opened up in only one direction, so each local had to work the industries in the direction the local was moving.

I arrived in Durham, North Carolina for work at 9:00am. I already knew a lot of the train crews and agents that worked around Durham from going through there so much on the Raleigh jobs. I was introduced to the Norfolk Southern (NS) crew that I would be working with. The train crew was from the former Norfolk Southern Railway out of Raleigh, North Carolina. The Southern Railway train crew was home based in Goldsboro, North Carolina with the N. S. Engineer.

The two rail unions, Brotherhood of Locomotive Engineers (BLE) and the United Transportation Union (UTU) put these crews together for the convenience of the Southern Railway employees. The conductor and flagman on the Southern side lived near Goldsboro, North Carolina. The engineer assigned to the Goldsboro local were closer to Spencer, North Carolina and thereby assigned to Durham, North Carolina. The Norfolk Southern engineer was assigned with the Southern train crew in Goldsboro and the Norfolk Southern train crew was assigned with the Southern engineer in Durham, North Carolina. This was very confusing, but that is the way it was.

The conductor I was working with was Harry Watson, an older man with the same personality traits as the old, grouchy conductors on our mainline. He was a very knowledgeable man, though. Ronnie and Butch were the head end brakeman and flagman, respectively. There was a different attitude in the way this crew worked then what I was used to with my former crews. Everything seemed to move in slow motion, including the train crew. When we had to talk on the radio, we had to precede every conversation with "Southern Railway", like "Southern Railway Train 64 calling Durham Yard". Conductor Watson started calling me "Southern Joe" and from that time on everyone called me "Southern Joe".

On the Raleigh jobs, we rarely got on overtime. However, on the Goldsboro local, making overtime is what these guys lived for. We usually worked 12 hours a day. From the time the engineer gets on the engine, until he gets off of the engine, he is always working. The ground crew however, when they are finished work in on the ground, they get up on the engine or caboose and ride to the next working stop.

Out of Durham, North Carolina train number 64 worked all the industries on double track between Cary, North Carolina and Raleigh, North Carolina. There was a cement company in Cary, Cary wholesale company, which was a beer distributor, Gregory Poole (heavy machinery), North Carolina transportation department, and Dillard Paper Company that we had to switch before getting into Raleigh. It usually took an hour or two to do all of the work on double track. All of these cars that we switched out worse than all in a track in the Raleigh yard, along with the cars designated for Raleigh.

The track going into Gregory Poole was so sharp that often times, the sixty feet long flat cars would derail going in to the industry. The flat cars carried heavy equipment like bulldozers. When these cars derailed, we had to call the shop people to re-rail the cars. The car usually would derail right on a road crossing and we would block traffic using that road. It would normally take an hour or so to re-rail the car. We went on duty in Durham, North Carolina at 8am, and by the time we got to Raleigh, North Carolina it was noon or so.

At Cary Wholesale there were usually damaged pallets of beer that we asked for and usually received. Nothing was wrong with the beer; just the cans were bent up a little bit. We put some of the beer in the coolers to cool down and the rest we set aside to take to the hotel when we got to Goldsboro, North Carolina later that night. Although it was against the rules, it sure was good on hot days to have a cold beer with lunch after leaving Raleigh, North Carolina. On one hot day, we stopped by a restaurant in Clayton, North Carolina to have lunch. While I was ordering my food, the cook glanced at my T-shirt. The slogan on my T-shirt read "Swing both ways and you'll never go home alone." After reading my T-shirt, the cook did a double take at me and went back to cooking. I always liked keeping people on their toes.

Normally, from Raleigh, North Carolina we would go to Selma, North Carolina where we met the other local. Unless otherwise specified in the train orders, train 63 would take the siding in Selma, while train 64 would be on the main line. Train 64, after crossing the interlocking for the CSX, which was the main line from Jacksonville, Florida to Richmond, Virginia, would stop to set all interchange cars for the CSX Transportation. The track we set the cars off in what is called the Pinner's Point lead. The interchange cars would go to Virginia by CSX.

After leaving Selma yard for Raleigh yard, the tracks were not kept up and became deteriorated. The company kept two tracks in Selma yard maintained enough to meet another train and do some switching on the train. If it was time for lunch, we would pull down the mainline so the other train could leave. After applying brakes on the train, we would set the engines free, go through the siding, and go up town to the house track where we parked the engines to go eat lunch.

After parking the engines, we walked two blocks to the restaurant. After being on the engine for about six to eight hours, it felt good to get off of it and stretch my legs. On hot days, I would get something cool to drink and something light to eat. In the winter time, I would get a bowl of soup or a hot meal to warm up. But, the main reason for taking lunch was to take a break from railroading to clear my mind.

When we left Princeton, North Carolina, we went to Goldsboro, North Carolina where we had to get permission from our dispatcher to occupy the limits of Carolina Power and Light (CPL). The Seaboard Coast line had trackage rights in this area also, because both Southern Railway and the Seaboard Coast line delivered coal to CPL. Each end of the Carolina Power and Light limits had a stop sign to stop at and a phone box to call the dispatcher for permission to use those limits. The conductor would usually try to get permission for these limits while we were in Selma, North Carolina. Then, all we had to do was to stop at the stop sign and then proceed on into Goldsboro, North Carolina.

When we got through with lunch, we would get the engines back out of the house track, go back through the siding, and couple back up to our train to continue on to Goldsboro, NC. The next stop was usually in Princeton, North Carolina. We would get five to ten cars out of the rock track and place whatever empty cars we had back into the track. Just beyond Princeton, North Carolina we had to switch out the cars in a feed mill. It was quite a nasty place to work. In the summer, it could be up to 100 degrees around this area. The flies were so bad in the feed mill; I had to close the engine windows to prevent the inside from being covered up with flies.

When we left Princeton, we went to Goldsboro, NC where we had to get permission from our dispatcher to occupy the limits of Carolina Power and Light (CPL). The CSX had track rights in this area also because both Southern Railway and CSX delivered coal to CPL. Each end of the CPL limits had a stop sign and a phone box to call the dispatcher for permission to use those limits. The conductor would usually try to get permission for the CPL limits when we were in Selma, North Carolina. When we had permission, all we had to do was stop at the stop sign and proceed on into Goldsboro, North Carolina .

The phone boxes at every station in dark territory were a step above the telegraph system. We had a control power switch we had to switch on and then speak to the dispatcher, if the line was not busy. The telephone lines were along the right of way from Greensboro, North Carolina all the way to Goldsboro, 130 miles away. If a tree fell on the lines and broke them, we would have no communication with the dispatcher. We would stop near a place with a real telephone and call the dispatcher collect. Most certainly, this was before cell phones.

At the start of the CPL limits, all the way to Goldsboro, the speed limit was 10 mph. The start of CPL limits was at Mile Post 124.5 and Goldsboro was at Miles Post 130. By the way, Durham was a Mile Post 55 and Raleigh was at Mile Post eighty. East Durham (Mile Post 58) was where we started out and to Goldsboro was only 72 miles. That makes us aware of why these jobs are called slow or dead freight trains.

Goldsboro yard was very small. It was comprised of several short tracks. When we terminated our train in Goldsboro with 40 to 60 cars, we filled up every track end to end. When we were down to just our engines, we went to the engine track, shut the engines down, locked them, and went to the yard office to register off duty. Another 12 hour day completed. The conductor, who had been in the yard office since we arrived at Goldsboro, called a taxi for us to go to the hotel.

It seemed to me that if the company would have put the night crew on duty before we spent two hours putting the train away, the crew could have taken the train on the mainline and left with it. As it was, the outbound crew spent a couple of hours putting the train back together before leaving for New Bern, North Carolina. It just didn't make good sense. Of course, when we mentioned something like that, the mismanagement officials would say, "You just don't see the big picture."

We went to the hotel front office, registered, and went to our rooms. I was normally too tired to eat, so I would get some ice, get comfortable, have a few drinks and watch television. I would have my choice of maybe seven to ten television stations. Goldsboro, North Carolina was home or Seymour Johnson Air Force Base. There was a night club in the hotel next to where we stayed and some of the guys went there to party.

It was in this timeframe, I bought a Subaru hatchback so I could leave the Volkswagen in Goldsboro, North Carolina. That way I could go back home to Raleigh, North Carolina every night and not stay in the hotel in Goldsboro, North Carolina. After all, it was only one hour away. Monday's, Wednesdays and Fridays we went to Goldsboro, North Carolina and Tuesday's, Thursdays and Saturdays we went back to Durham, North Carolina. After starting the engines, we would get the caboose over the last switch of the yard, so we could start shoving out the cuts of cars that made up our train. With so many are crossings so close together, we had to shove the train clear of the crossings so traffic would not be backed up. When we got all of our cars together, we would make a brake test of the cars and leave town.

In Goldsboro, North Carolina, we had to switch out a beer distributor and pick up the Seaboard Coastline interchange cars. Then, we picked up whatever coal cars for CPL that we may have set off the day before for spotting. There would be empty coal cars we had to pick up when we arrived at CPL. there were five tracks at CPL, two CSX tracks, two Southern tracks, and a main line. We pulled our cars into an empty track, and shoved the empty ones out onto the mainline. The flagman of our train had to ride the rear of the coal cars three and one half miles back out to the mainline. While going by some mobile homes one day, we spotted a marijuana plant growing in the window of the home.

By the time we left the Goldsboro CPL limits, we could have up to 100 cars. Any time we picked up any cars, we would have to make a brake test on the cars air brake system that we added to the train. We could do this on the cars separately, or when we coupled up to the train. All the work around Goldsboro, North Carolina would usually take about three to four hours.

When we left Goldsboro, North Carolina, our next stop would be Selma, North Carolina where we normally would take the siding and clear the mainline. If the other train was not there, we did whatever work we had to do around Selma, like pick up the connection from the Seaboard Coastline and waited for train 64 to meet us. When train 64 arrived, we copied orders to proceed on to Raleigh, North Carolina.

Often times, we would be held out of Raleigh because of other train movements. Some of these delays would be up to two or three hours. After these delays, we would be lucky to make it into Durham, North Carolina within our twelve hour working limit. By the Federal Railroad Administration service law, we could not work over 12 hours.

We normally had to set cars off at Raleigh and picked up cars for Durham, North Carolina. There were two industries we had to work after leaving Raleigh, North Carolina. In Clegg, North Carolina, there was a gravel pit and a wood manufacturer. The track for the latter had a very sharp curve in it and often times the railcars derailed because of its curvature. The speed limit in this industry was five mph.

After we left Clegg, we would go into Durham yard, that is, if we were not held out of the yard. More often than not, we would be on duty 12 hours going west as we did going east. On Saturday, we would try to make as short of a day as possible, so the weekend would be a little longer. The hours were long, but the paydays were very good.

While I was on the Goldsboro Local, I hit two vehicles with the train. Well, kind of like it. One of them actually ran into the engine. The land is pretty flat on the eastern side of North Carolina so we could see the crossings from a long way, if we were on straight track. We were coming into Goldsboro, North Carolina on a clear day and I saw this car coming to the crossing about a half of a mile away. All I could do was sound the whistle approaching the crossing.

I was steadily sounding the whistle approaching the crossing as I watched the car coming to the crossing to see if he was going to slow down or stop for the train. He didn't do either. He ran into the side of the engine right beneath me, while I was still at 25 MPH. Of course, the headlines in the next day's newspaper read, "Train Hits Car." That is the feeling of the public, is that the train chases the cars in an open field to hit them. No! We travel on rails and it is up to the drivers of the vehicles to yield to the train. The train outweighs any vehicle four thousand to one.

The other vehicle, so to speak, was a farm harvester. I was coming out of Goldsboro, North Carolina at a speed of 10 MPH, for that was the listed track speed. There was a lot of farm land around Goldsboro, so I saw the combine coming to the crossing at a slow speed. I thought that was an indication of him preparing to stop before the tracks for the train. I was wrong. He was on the tracks before he looked for the train. With our combined slow speeds, all we did was knock the combine over.

Dixie and I moved out of the mobile home park and bought a patio home across Capital Boulevard from where we did live. It was a two bedroom, two bathrooms house and better than where we were. I really liked being in North Raleigh. In the evenings, I would ride a bicycle around the neighborhood to keep in shape. There is nothing that would put weight on me as quick as inactivity for sitting in the engineers' seat all day.

As I was riding around the neighborhood one evening, I met a woman riding her bike also. We became friends and I found out she was from Salisbury, North Carolina as I was. Her name was Millie Massey and we played golf together about every Sunday. Dixie, Millie and I were on bowling teams together also. We socialized together a lot. Millie worked for an insurance company and just lived four houses from Dixie and I. It must have been fate by meeting Millie in Raleigh, North Carolina and we were both from Salisbury, North Carolina.

When we went golfing, Millie and I would stop at one of the fast food places to get breakfast. I never had any luck getting my order correct from fast food orders at the drive thru. I would order the same thing, usually a sausage and egg biscuit with milk to drink. One time

I receive my biscuit as ordered, but I received a hash brown patty with a straw and no milk. I asked Millie if I was supposed to snort the hash brown through my nose with the straw.

After that episode, I told Millie I was going to tell the drive thru people just give me any kind of order because I would not get what I ordered anyway. The next time, that is what I did. I told them to just give me some kind of sandwich it didn't matter for I wouldn't get what I wanted, charge me a fair price, and I would be on my way. I had no problem with my order that day.

Dixie and I ordered chicken one evening, two three-piece dinners. When I got home, I found that we had two - two-piece dinners. I called up the chicken place and asked them, "How many pieces of chicken are in a three piece chicken dinner?" When they told me three, I drove back to get two more pieces. Of course, when I got back home, my mashed potatoes were cold.

Most of the time, the train crew members and I shared rides with each other to work and back home. One trip when we arrived at Goldsboro, North Carolina, I noticed that my Volkswagen was not where I parked it that trip before. I found out that it was stolen. After filing a police report, the conductor and I rode the bus back to Raleigh. I ended up having to buy another Subaru for transportation back and forth to work. The police found my Volkswagen in Richmond, Virginia. I had to go to Richmond to get my car. Someone had broken the steering locking mechanism and hotwired the car. The Volkswagen was stuck in first gear and I guess that is the reason they had abandoned it. The policemen showed me how to hotwire my car to get it started and I drove to a repair shop where the mechanic fixed the gears. I drove it back to Raleigh, North Carolina and sold it soon afterward.

The Goldsboro job was a good paying job, but the Burlington Local was going to move its home terminal to Durham, North Carolina. I bid on the job and I was the highest bidder (in seniority). I thought it would be a better job, plus the fact I would be working with an all Southern Railway crew. Bronnie Morgan was the conductor, whose nicked name was "Bigfoot" for obvious reasons. Another big guy, Dave, was the brakeman and Heggie was the flagman. We worked all the industries between Durham, North Carolina and Gibsonville, North Carolina.

We still had flagging rules to go by, so every stop we had to place torpedoes on the rail one and a half miles before we were to stop to switch out the industries. We were paid for ten hours work no matter how long we worked and we didn't get on overtime until we were on duty for over ten hours. We didn't drag our feet on this job like the way the guys did on the Goldsboro job. The earlier we got off, the better it was for us. Because of the experience we all had at railroading, we operated like a well-oiled machine. We had some ninety plus years combined railroad seniority in our crew. And besides that, I could still be home every night.

Bronnie moved from Salisbury, North Carolina to Raleigh like I did. I thought he was following me (No, just kidding). When Bronnie got married in Raleigh, I was his best man at the wedding. We just had a good time working together. We got the work done fast and efficient, and then went home to spend time with our families. Sometimes there was little work to be done, and we were back in the yard and off duty in four hours or less. We still got paid for ten hours, so it was a very good job.

On the Burlington Local we had to make a side trip to Carrboro, North Carolina once or twice a week to deliver coal to the energy plant at the University of North Carolina. With only one engine, we hauled ten cars of coal to Carrboro and brought back ten empties to the main line. The run around track in Carrboro only held ten cars, so it was just enough room to run around the cars to get the engine on the other end of the cars for the return trip to the main line.

On one of these trips to Carrboro, I had yet another collision with a vehicle. A woman was driving a Volkswagen van approaching a crossing I was approaching. I was going ten MPH for the whole line had a speed of ten MPH on the track. She didn't look for the train until the last second. She then put the brake on so hard and turned the wheel to the left real hard to avoid hitting the train that she turned the van over on its side and slid into the side of the engine.

When her van hit the engine, the vehicle broke the air pipe that supplied air to our air brake system. As a result, all the air in the reservoir leaked out and we lost all of our air brakes and we started rolling back down hill. I jumped out the door real quick to put the engine hand brake on, while the brakeman went back to the train to apply as many hand brakes on the cars to stop the train from rolling backwards. It is very rare that collisions disable the engines from operating. We had to call the shop at Durham, North Carolina to repair the engine air line before we could go any farther.

On another trip going through Mebane, North Carolina, I had another collision with a car. It appeared at first he was stalled on the track. When I kept sounding the whistle for him to move or get out of the car, he just looked at me. I will never forget the passionless expression on his face when the train ran into the passenger side of his car at 49 MPH. He died on the way to the hospital. The conductor, Scott Shoaf, told me that his daughter was sitting on a school bus behind him and she witnessed the whole thing.

With the older engineers retiring on the Danville district, I was getting close in seniority to having a main line carded run. A carded job worked four days straight and then had one day off. This routine cycled through weekends and holidays no matter what. They normally worked the hotshots and were paid 168 miles from Spencer, North Carolina to Monroe, Virginia (equivalent to 1 and ½ days pay). I knew I could not work the carded runs from Raleigh, North Carolina, so when I won the bid for a carded run, Dixie and I moved to Greensboro, North Carolina. Dixie didn't like Salisbury so that is the reason we moved to Greensboro. In 1985, after being an engineer for eleven years, I became one of the main line engineers.

The line from Monroe, Virginia to Spencer, North Carolina was made famous in the song "The Wreck of the Old 97" by Johnny Cash. In one line the song states, "It's a mighty rough road from Lynchburg to Danville lying on a three mile grade". From the top of White Oak Mountain to Dan River though is ten miles. This referred to the grade off of White Oak Mountain going into Danville, Virginia. The story goes on to say the air brakes failed on the mail train and turned over because of excessive speed around a curve. Some crew members of that train lost their lives in that wreck that occurred in 1903.

Chapter Fourteen-Life on the Main Line

The biggest down side to the carded runs was living in a dormitory in Monroe, Virginia. I had to get a cabinet that was lockable for canned goods and dry goods, as well as a locker to put into the refrigerator for perishables. I emphasize locks, because if I left any food unlocked in the kitchens, the thieves would think you are leaving food unlocked for them.

Normally, the same crews worked together, so we would plan meals together to eat supper. If we were lucky, we could be called for one of the two hot shots leaving Monroe, Virginia for Spencer, North Carolina the next day. A lot of the guys had old cars at the dormitory, so they could drive into Lynchburg, Virginia to eat supper. Most of the time, they went to the K & W cafeteria to eat rather than cooking. The owners of the cars collected $.50 from each person for gas money to ride with them to eat. That was not bad considering the trip was 20 miles round-trip.

When it came time to remodel the dormitory, we stayed at the Holiday Inn in Lynchburg. There were much better beds to sleep in and a TV in each room and we did not have to "bunk with anyone else". On the downside, we had to eat at the restaurant in the hotel, so it was more expensive on meal expenses. Those people who had cars could still go into Lynchburg, Virginia to eat. But the best part was not being at the dormitory.

There were three hot shots going north to Monroe and only two hot shots coming back south to Spencer. The other train that was called in the morning in Monroe, Virginia was a dead freight. The crews were supposed to be called in order of arriving and Monroe, but I was convinced the yard master or crew caller abused that rule. We could be called for train 159 (the dead freight) ten minutes before a hotshot was called to leave. The dead freight would be on duty ten to twelve hours while the hotshot would be on duty about six hours or less. That situation would be just playing favorites with the crews, because anyone would know the dead freight crew could not even get their engines together before the hotshot would run around them in the yard. Just spike work and real asinine is all it was. Sometimes, they would call the dead freight before both hotshots going south, and the crew of the dead freight would be run around by two crews. It was always a guess who would be called for what train going back to Spencer, North Carolina.

The main line engineers had to be "radio train" qualified. A radio train had an engine that had radio equipment to send a radio signal to a special radio car sending radio signals to a couple of engines coupled with the radio car in the middle of the train. Once set up, I could have three engines on the head of the train with two engines near the middle of the train applying the same power. Instead of too much power on the head of the train, the engines were split up to make the weight of the train distributed, so it would run and operate like a shorter, lighter train.

The radio train had to have all the engines working and was difficult to set up. The mechanical department worked with the engineer to set up the radio car and engines, both the master engines (the ones on the head of the train) and the slave units (the ones in the middle of the train) working in continuity with each other. If everything went well after setting up the slave units, the train ran and operated like a much lighter, shorter train. The brakes on the slave engines would apply the brakes both ways through the train line, so air brakes would go on quicker and release much quicker.

The weather was more severe in Virginia than it was in North Carolina in the winter time, so we had to dress appropriately. It snowed a lot more in Virginia than it did in the Carolinas. The interchange for the Norfolk and Western Railway empty coal hoppers was at Hurt, Virginia. Hurt, Virginia was by Altavista, Virginia. When a freight train arrived at Hurt, Virginia, the switcher assigned there would assist them to the deliver the cars to the Norfolk and Western. The switcher would be finished for the night when they delivered the empties, so they tried to hustle the move as much as they could so they could get off earlier. On one of these occasions, when the freight train crew cut away from the cars, the conductor of the switcher "bottled the air" to save time from pumping the brakes off. He turned both angle cocks so the air would not escape.

"Bottling the air" means blocking the air on each end of the cars by turning the angle cocks, thereby trapping the air in the train. However, with the new ABD brakes, the air could pump the brakes off and allow the train to roll down the hill. Anyway, while the cars were sitting there with no engine attached to them, the air brakes pumped off and the cars started to roll away. The forty or so cars started delivering themselves to the Norfolk and Western. The conductor tried to catch the cars, but he could not. The cars ran into another track full of cars and derailed making a big pile of cars. Needless to say, it is "against the rules" to bottle the air, so the conductor was suspended from service for a while.

Being fired from the railroad was actually being suspended from service as punishment for violating the rules. When you were caught violating the rules, or when you had a foul-up like a derailment or collision, we had to go to an investigation to see who was at fault. After the investigation, if the company thought we were guilty as charged, we would be suspended from service for a determined length of time.

For this reason, we had what was called hit-and-run insurance. This was basically an insurance policy that paid us while we were "out of service". Along with the unemployment we collected, most people made more money being out of service than they did when they were actually working. If the insurance paid well enough, it was like having a vacation from the railroad.

I was suspended from service several times. While I was off the railroad, I was a carpenter helper for Tom Graham. He paid me ten dollars an hour and I knew I made more money "being fired" than I did when I was working. I met Tom in 1972 when I first moved to Salisbury, North Carolina. I was living in a duplex and he was building a house right behind the house I lived in. We became good friends and through the years, I helped him build a bunch of houses. He is a very good carpenter. In fact, I contracted him to build my house in later years.

One winter day started out as any other, but soon turned into one of the worst trips I ever had. Bobby Nichols was my brakeman. After we loaded up the engines with our bags, ice, water, and supplies, we started out of the shop. Approaching the derail, I tried to slow up the engines with the engine brake and I noticed the engines were not slowing down. I applied more engine brake and then I noticed there was no air showing on the brake gauge. We were getting closer to the derail, so I had to open the door to get to the engine hand brake to stop the engines.

It was just starting to snow and was very windy as I opened the door to stop the engines. The wind blew my safety glasses and the hood to my parka off of my head. When I got the engines stopped, luckily before going over the derail, I found out the diesel shop had not cut the air back into the trucks of the engine after testing them. Both of the engines had no air supplied to the brakes. After that incident, I always check to make sure I had brakes on the engines before leaving the shop. But, this was just the start of our bad trip.

The snow continued to fall as we got the train together and left the yard. Sam Ball was the flagman on this trip. When Sam loaded up on the caboose with all the clothes and food he carried with him, he loaded up to live there a while.

The further north we travelled, the snow was coming down harder and eventually covered the ground as well as the tracks. The snow accumulated up to around fourteen inches with snow drifts up to five feet. The engines we had were equipped with a radar screen on the front trucks preventing the engines from wheel slipping. If the radar didn't determine you needed power, the computer would not allow the engines to load up any further. However, with the snow covering the screen, the computer wouldn't allow the engines to load up even when I needed them to load.

We only had around 6,600 tons with about 75 railroad cars, but we stalled in Chatham, Virginia going uphill. When we stopped, the train started rolling back down the hill. I put the train into emergency, but to my amazement, the train was still rolling back down the hill. I had to reset the power control switch, put the engines in number one power, with the train in full emergency just to stay on the hill.

There was another train behind us on the same track, so we told him over the radio to hold back just in case we started rolling back again. Bobby had to get under the engine to clean the snow off of the radar screen, so we could have power. After doing this several times, we managed to finally make it up the hill.

What was happening, I determined, was the snow was building up on the brake pads of the rail cars melting, and then turning into ice rendering the brakes useless. We had to meet Amtrak at the end of double track at the end of a three mile grade, so I stopped the train on top of the hill, for I was afraid I would not be able to stop the train at the stop signal before going into the single track.

When Amtrak came by us, all we saw was the lead engine of his train, for the snow covered up the rest of his train. After Amtrak passed, I eased around the curve with the train to see if we had a green signal and we proceeded on to Monroe, Virginia. I was going real slowly into the station at Monroe, Virginia so I would be able to stop to change crews, but I still went by where I wanted to stop, because the brakes were not as effective as they normally would have been without the ice on the brakes.

The snow was still falling and the wind was making big snow drifts. When Bobby was making his way through the snow to the dorm, he fell into one of these snow drifts up to his shirt pocket. We really looked like snow bunnies going into the dorm.

The outbound crew had as much trouble with the train as we did and the engines would not even pull the train up to the station to let Sam off of the caboose. Bobby and ate something went to our dorm rooms to go to sleep. When I got up the next morning and went into the TV room, Sam was just then coming into the dorm. He had to sleep on the cab the whole night. He had plenty of food with him, so he didn't go hungry.

All the trains were having trouble with ice building up on the brake shoes. One of the engineers was questioned about his inability to move the train, so he asked the Chief Dispatcher "Are you aware of the conditions we are working in?" The Dispatcher replied, "I am well aware about the conditions you are working in!" I find that hard to believe, because the dispatcher's office was in Greensboro, North Carolina on the second floor of a climate controlled building and the only snow they encountered was walking through the parking lot! The trains were running in two feet of snow!

I was on train number 173 from Monroe, Virginia to Spencer, North Carolina one day with Billy McCall and Frank Robinson serving as the conductor and brakeman, respectively. We were coming around a curve in Thomasville, North Carolina traveling at fifty MPH. The crossing at the time had only cross bucks to denote the existence of the railroad.

Billy saw a car trying to beat the train. It was a Volkswagen, no less. We were going to hit the car, so Billy yelled at me to put the train into emergency. I immediately felt the impact of the engine slamming into the car. The train knocked the car into a train signal and knocked it down. I was trying my best to stop the train as quick as I could, but it was still one mile before the train came to a complete stop.

Billy and Frank went back to the collision as fast as they could to help out the people in the car. When they came back to the engine about an hour or so later, Billy told me that a three year old girl was dead in the passenger seat. That collision really upset me emotionally. We didn't talk much for the rest of the trip. I guess we were all thinking about what happened. When I got off the train, I went to a store and bought two quarts of beer. But, they could not drown out the memory of what happened, and neither has time healed the wounds I felt on that day.

The father of this girl was 24 years old trying to beat the train and ended his daughter's life. But, I remember when she was to begin high school. I remember when she was to go to the Junior-Senior prom. I remember when she was to graduate from high school, but her life was over before it began, and I felt responsible. There was nothing I could do.

I could never understand why drivers take such chances with their lives, trying to beat the train. Most trains will not have the crossing blocked that long of time. For the sake of a few minutes, people will risk their lives as well as others in the vehicles for no reason at all. I will never understand it.

I first met Bill Reynolds when I took an empty coal hopper train to Hurt, Virginia. He was a company clerk at the time and eventually he switched jobs to become a brakeman and then qualified as an engineer. We became friends and remained friends through our changes of addresses through the years. When I was living in Raleigh, North Carolina, and he came in off the train, he came over my house to visit. He was renting a room from my first wife, Pam, in Spencer, North Carolina. At least, I thought he was a friend.

While Dixie and I were living in Greensboro, North Carolina, my daughter Peggy wanted us to come to Salisbury, North Carolina for a visit. Pam was living in an apartment complex near the Salisbury Mall.

When we got there, Peggy told me, "Dad, I have to tell you something, but you have to promise me you won't do anything." I asked her what it was. Again, she said I have to promise not to do anything. I said okay, I promise, so what is this about?

She told me while I was living in Raleigh, North Carolina when she was between nine and eleven years old, Bill Reynolds had raped and molested her. I was devastated when she told me of this secret that she had held within herself for years. I went into the bathroom to conceal my crying. Dixie came in to comfort me and after I came out of the bathroom, I called the call office of the railroad and ask them where Bill Reynolds was at that very time. I intended to go find him and kill him on the spot, breaking my promise to my daughter. Peggy blocked the door with her body so I could not leave. She told me she had talked to the police and she was going to have a wired microphone on to trick Bill into confessing to his ill deeds, so the court could prosecute him and then put him in jail. She told me she wanted to do this and that I would only go to jail for killing someone and she would lose me.

I finally calmed down and try to think of Peggy and what she had endured. She had to drop out of Western Carolina University in her sophomore year, because of the emotional burden she was enduring. The hate and discontent I felt toward Bill was enormous.

Although, no one confronted me directly on the railroad, the word got around to my fellow railroad workers what had happened. On one trip coming into Spencer Yard from the north end with light engines (no train), I heard Bill Reynolds on the radio coming in from the south end heading for diesel shop, where we were going. The conductor and flagman usually got off at the pull back shack to get a ride to the yard office to put off duty and go home. It was normal procedure for only the brakeman and engineer to take the engines to the diesel shop, but all the crewmembers stay on going to the shop.

When I realized that all the crew members were still on the train, I asked, "What are all you guys still doing on here?" The conductor replied, "We are on here to protect you." I said, "I don't need any protection, I'm going to cut the S.O.B. up into pieces and stuff him into an empty locker." Britton said, "That is what I am afraid of, so we are going to keep you out of trouble." When we got the engines into the shop, I went to the engineer's locker room looking for him, but he was gone. I fully intended to cause him some bodily harm.

Some months later, Peggy met up with Bill at a local teen's hangout wearing a wire the police provided for her. During the conversation, Bill had pretty much admitted what he had done. The police brought him into the station to question him about the events that took place, which he denied. However, after the police played the tape for him, he just dropped his head knowing he had been caught. He pleaded guilty to three charges of child molestation and rape charges. The judge sentenced him to six years on each count. My math adds that up to 18 years, but he was released after ten years. At least Peggy got some justice out of it. Bill lost his job on the railroad, because if you have a felony, you cannot work for the company.

There were a lot of changes going on in this time period. The dormitory in Monroe, Virginia was shut down and the new terminal was in Lynchburg, Virginia. There had been rumors of this happening for some time. New asphalt had been replaced in the parking lot in Monroe, Virginia and soon thereafter, sure enough, they closed the terminal down. The good thing about that was the crews were being lodged at hotels instead of the antiquated dormitory in Monroe, Virginia.

When the Southern Railroad merged with the Norfolk and Western in 1980, the company built a connection track at Altavista, Virginia to accommodate trains coming off of our main line to their main line to Roanoke, Virginia. This track was used to deliver the empty coal hoppers to Roanoke, Virginia and then on to Bluefield, West Virginia for reloading. The coal trains would use this track for connections to the south.

Interdivisional runs were established that went from Linwood, North Carolina to Manassas, Virginia, a total of 296 miles. These runs were some of the highest paying jobs and only those people with the oldest seniority were on them. Now, instead of seeing the end of the trip coming into Monroe, Virginia, we had another 130 miles to go for the end of the trip. We also had runs going to Alexandria, Virginia. These were piggy-back trains with containerized freight and truck trailers on flat cars.

On one of these trips north of Charlottesville, Virginia, my conductor told me they had a "Yard of the Month" in the town of Barboursville, Virginia. Bronnie Morgan and I had pretty landscapes yards wherever we lived. The yard he pointed out to me when we went by, could not be seen for all the ground was covered with junk and trash. At night, you could see a bug-zapper hanging on the inside of the house! The people who lived there had no grass visible to cut. Some of the backyards we went by were interesting, and others were not.

Not only did I have to learn more track layout by getting qualified on the Washington District, but I also operated trains through very historic places. I went through Charlottesville, Virginia and campus of the University of Virginia. Close by, was Monticello, the home of Thomas Jefferson, the third president of the United States, first Secretary of State, and second Vice President.

I also went by Montpelier, which was the home of James Madison, who was fourth President of the United States. It is stated that he conceived his ideas of government while at Montpelier. He was given the title "Father of the Constitution" by his colleagues. James Madison married Dolley Payne Todd on September 15, 1794, after courting her for several months.

James Madison held the office of Secretary of State in the cabinet of President Thomas Jefferson. Madison sent James Monroe to complete the Louisiana Purchase from Napoleon of France. He also funded the Lewis and Clark Expedition to purchase land west of the Mississippi for Americans to be able to travel west to the Pacific Ocean.

During his term in office, James Madison was one of the few presidents to lead a command in the field of battle. He failed to stop the British from invading Washington. Dolley Madison assisted in removing papers, documents, and a picture of George Washington from the White House, before the British burned the White House and the Capitol Building

After Washington, the British Navy went on to Fort McHenry in Baltimore. They failed to win there, but the battle inspired Francis Scott Key to write the "Star Spangled Banner", which became our national anthem. After his second term ended in 1817, James and Dolley Madison retired to Montpelier.

North of Manassas, Virginia, I went by Bull Run which was the landmark of the first major battles in the Civil War. There was a first and second Bull Run. When I went by there, I also thought about how it was said, "The River ran red from the blood of soldiers killed in battle." I was always interested in history and traveling along these historical places sure did un-nerve me.

My brother, Lonnie Harris, did a genealogy of our ancestors. He asked me to see what I could find out in the library at the University of North Carolina at Greensboro. I found out that some of our ancestors had fought in the Revolutionary War, as well as the Civil War. Some had been Commissioners in Bladen County in North Carolina. I tracked back as far as a William Cain (1700-1781), who was given 640 acres around 1734 by King George of England. It was very interesting stuff. I found a blemish in our family tree, though. I found a James Cain who deserted in the Civil War, after being shot in the foot. Oh well, I might have done the same thing.

Triple Crown trains were also established that originated in Hagerstown, Maryland going to Atlanta, Georgia at the end of our division. Our run was from Lynchburg, Virginia to Greenville, South Carolina (300 miles). Triple Crown trains were truck trailers that were placed on train truck wheels to accommodate the trailers to ride on the rail. The trains were pulled by only one engine. The trains were so light that they could run uphill and downhill at 60 MPH. Heaven forbid that you had trouble with that engine, for we would be dead in the water.

With the home terminal in Lynchburg, Virginia, we had to drive there from Linwood, North Carolina which was 150 miles. Oftentimes, we had to get up at three in the morning to see what time the train was going to be in Lynchburg to make the three hour drive to meet the train. There was only a conductor and engineer on the crew. The crews were being downsized to save on labor costs. The only trains that had a brakeman on them were the local freight and switcher engines that had more work on them.

I decided to go on one of the Roanoke runs because it paid more than the Lynchburg runs. Of course, I had to learn more of "The lay of the land" going to Roanoke. One guy told me, "It's no problem; it is 40 miles, four tunnels, and flat." That was true, but when I got into Roanoke, what a maze of tracks running everywhere and signals for the tracks everywhere. It was difficult to tell what signal governed what track. We needed a road map to figure out where we were and where we were going. It was maddening.

Going to Roanoke on a train was a real adventure. We could make the trip in about eight hours, but we were held out of the yard so long that we were usually on duty for twelve hours or more. We could only work 12 hours by the hours of service rule, but some trips by the time we were off the train and at the hotel we stayed at, we could have been on duty for 12-16 hours or more. Talk about a long day.

The regular train going to Roanoke was Train 128, which was called in the evening seven days a week. It arrived in Roanoke sometime in the morning. When I first started going to Roanoke, we stayed at the Jefferson Inn in downtown Roanoke. On one side of the hotel, rooms were provided for women going to beauty school, and on the other side of the hotel was where the railroad men stayed. It is no wonder why the hotel had a guard to keep the two separated!

Train 128 usually stopped at Greensboro, North Carolina and Danville, Virginia to set off cars and pick up more cars going to Roanoke. We had to pick up these cars in station order, so sometimes we could be holding onto 60 to 80 cars to do the work. On one trip like this, we were at Greensboro for two and one half hours while it was raining very hard the whole time. When the train crew got back on the engines to leave Greensboro, they were totally soaking wet from head to toe.

When we stopped at the end of double track to wait for Amtrak, my conductor, Britton, took off his clothes to hang them up near the heaters to dry them. While he was sitting there in only his underwear, he asked if I would take the revised train list back to the second engine to give a copy to the brakeman and flagman. I was the driest of the train crew, so I did. When I got back to the engine where the crew was, I saw that they also had stripped down to their underwear drying their clothes. As I was going back to the lead engine, I was thinking, "I sure hope nothing happens tonight for the officials to get up on our train. Everyone was down to their underwear except me!" It sure didn't look good.

When we got off duty in Roanoke, we usually went to a restaurant to eat. It amazed me that at six in the morning the cafes opened and were serving beer at that time. Being that it was at the end of our work day, we usually drank some beers to relax before going to bed.

Roanoke Valley is comprised of three cities; Roanoke, Salem, and Vinton. From most of the valley, we could see the 50 feet tall star that was on top of Mill Mountain. If we were on top of the mountain, we could see most of the valley below. It was very beautiful to watch at dusk when the lights of the city started coming on. We could also see the rail trains slowly moving through the cities coming in and out of town.

On one trip when one of my friends went out to party, he hooked up with a woman and went home with her. When he got up the next morning and needed a ride to get back to the hotel, he called the manager of the restaurant to go pick him up. She asked, "Where are you, Neil?" He replied, "I don't know where I am, but I can see the star on Mill Mountain from where I'm at." That narrowed it down to a ten mile radius. That was funny.

We could also go to Roanoke via Lynchburg going over the Blue Ridge Mountains. We could not take heavy trains over the mountain, for the engines would not pull the trains over it. That was what I called the scenic route, it was a pretty run.

Oftentimes, if there was more freight moving south than north, we deadheaded in a taxi to Roanoke to get a train. We either went to the yard to get on the train, or we went to the hotel to take eight hours rest before getting called to go to work. If we were at the away-from-home-terminal for 16 hours off duty, we went on detention time, which was being paid for not going to work.

I think Frank Houston and I set a record on deadheading. We deadheaded to Roanoke for a train one day, and after being there 24 hours making eight hours detention time, they deadheaded us back to Linwood, North Carolina because there was no freight moving out of Roanoke. After being home for eight to ten hours, they deadheaded us back to Roanoke, Virginia. Then, after our rest was up, they finally called us for train ride instead of a taxi ride. Three consecutive deadheads, they were actually paying us to ride up and down the highway in a taxi cab.

At this time, the company was still running radio trains out of Roanoke, Virginia, because of the weight of the trains. The trains could be 12,000 to 13,000 tons. Putting the radio trains together in Roanoke was a real nightmare, because it took so long. I have been called for a radio train, went to work on it, and because of the failure to get them to work right, have to go back to the hotel for another eight hours rest. It was very frustrating to work four to six hours on a train, trying to leave the yard, and then because we didn't have enough time left to make the trip, the trainmaster sent us back to the hotel.

Of course the crew that relieved us loved it, all they had to do was make a brake test on the train and leave town. Everything seemed to move in slow motion in Roanoke, for no one got into a hurry. Whatever track we had to get to our train, it was a given, we would be blocked in by another train or have to wait for another train to come into yard before we left.

Sometimes, we were called for a power move, that is, to get a number of engines to a terminal where they needed the power. We would actually think, because they needed the power, we could have a short time on duty. Wrong! I had a set of 16 engines going to Roanoke from Linwood Yard. After putting my bag on the lead engine, I walked through the engine consist, got off the rear engine, and walked back to the lead engine. After getting off the engines in Roanoke, I walked by the entire consist of engines to get to the yard office. The trip took twelve hours to go 180 miles, and I walked further on that trip than the brakeman did!

With the merger with Norfolk and Western, we had train 159 going to Crewe, Virginia. That was another good paying job. One Road Forman remarked to me, "Crewe, Virginia is a perfect place for the railroad man to go to for the sake of his wife. There is nothing but the hotel that the railroad men go to for miles around. There is no trouble for him to get into." That was so true; it was a very boring place to be. Once we arrived at Lynchburg, Virginia, we still had about seventy miles to go to Crewe, Virginia. It was a long and boring run.

We went through Appomattox, Virginia, the site of Confederate General Robert E. Lee's surrender to Union General Ulysses S. Grant on April 9, 1865, signaling the end of the American Civil War. Virginia has a multitude of historic sites and I did some heavy thinking traveling through these sites.

I became Local Chairman of our lodge 375 and had to babysit the members. I had meetings with the Superintendent of the Division about all the engineers' welfare and job assignments. The major concern at the time was a shortage of engineers. I noticed the listing of the engineer positions on a sheet that the Superintendent had with him on a desk beside me. If all the engineers were available for work that were on the seniority list, with no one sick, out of service, or on vacation; we were still short about five engineers to fill jobs. I guess he wanted me make some engineers, but I could not do that. At one point, we were short on conductors, and I was asked by the trainmaster and the local chairman of the UTU, to cut the engineers extra board, so they would have more conductors. The engineers on the extra board were working about every day. I could not rationalize cutting men off the board to fill a shortage of conductors. It just didn't make good sense.

Working one job was not enough then, because the call office would call you on your off days to work some other job, because the railroad just didn't have enough people to work. I tried to be tactful and explain to the officers, "If we need 20 conductors and 20 engineers, but we only had ten of each, how many people do we need to operate the trains?" They still didn't get it. I guess they thought I was hiding engineers somewhere and wouldn't tell them where they were. If anyone had to be off for any reason, we could not, unless it was an emergency. Getting time off was becoming like an Act of Congress. They were checking the work history of the employees to see if they had too much time off. They told one engineer, "See, you were off on this day here." The engineer checked the date in his book and said, "Yes, I was held away from home in Roanoke, Virginia that day."

It didn't seem to bother the company if the employee had been up all day doing his "Homework", but if they called us for a job that was going to work all night, we had to go. Never mind about "Safety First" then, we just need a body on that train. Fatigue was becoming a very real problem and the railroads' answer to that was to show us a film about our "rest cycle", which didn't help our situation at all. I used to tell my train crew, "It makes me mad as hell to wake up and see my crew asleep." That did keep them awake for a little while.

I passed by one train one day and the other crew of that train noticed both of my crew members were asleep. The engineer said, "You're by yourself, aren't you Joe?" I looked over and saw both them asleep and I gave them hell. I told them as far as I was concerned, they could be replaced by a "No Smoking" sign.

Chapter Fifteen-The Unions

In 1985 the United Transportation Union (UTU) agreed in a contract with the carriers to reduce the pay of new hires by 15%. The new hires would get a 5% pay raise each year up to five years. Everyone hired after that year had to become an engineer as the need became necessary. This agreement tended to cause resentment in the new hires and they had an attitude of (them against us). As a result, the UTU stood for You-Took-Us.

There always seemed to be resentment between the Brotherhood of Locomotive Engineers (BLE) and the UTU. The BLE represented the engineers primarily and the UTU represented the trainmen and conductors primarily. However, both unions had both engineers and train crews in them. This resentment worked very well in the company's favor. The UTU negotiated the contracts for the brakemen and conductors and the BLE did the same for the engineers. Oddly enough, both international unions were in Cleveland, Ohio.

I became a member of the BLE in 1973 when I became a fireman. I was in Local 375 of the BLE. The Local 375 was chartered and held monthly meetings to discuss all the aspects concerning the operations, jobs and discrepancies of the brotherhood. We had officers of the union that directed the members. Some of the officers were; Local Chairman, President, Chaplin, and Secretary-Treasurer. The Local Chairman had to be a liaison between the union and the companies to establish jobs, settle claims against the company, and represent the members at investigations when held.

The Local Chairman position was a thankless job. No matter how he decided, there were people who disagreed with his decisions. Normally, these people were the ones that did not attend the meetings to vote on issues of the lodge. Rather than to take part in the process, it was much easier to complain on the decisions made. The attitude of "What's in it for me?"

When I was living in Greensboro, North Carolina, I was close enough to attend the meetings held in Spencer, North Carolina. A lot of members did not want to become local officers for a variety of reasons. There were a lot of responsibilities that came with being a union officer and most members wanted to stay away from it. However, they asked me if I would replace the Secretary-Treasurer, who was going to become the Local Chairman of the Division 375. I said I would and I received all of books and records of Division 375. I had to fill out monthly ledgers to account for the monies coming in and write checks for money going out as well as keeping minutes of the meetings I attended.

Along with the monthly ledgers, at the end of the year I had to submit a form to the government of all the assets and liabilities of the lodge. I guess because of the corruption in some unions, the government wanted to keep a check of the unions to confirm they were on the up and up. All of these records were filled by hand with a pencil and it usually took me the better part of a day or two per month to do all the work involved. These were not very small books either. They were about two feet wide and about one foot in height. I had an entry for every member and the amount of money deducted each month and broken down to where every cent of the money was going to.

I got separated from Dixie, so I moved to Rowan county so I wouldn't have far to go to work. I lived with my brother, Butch, and his wife Sue. It was a very small apartment and I eventually found an apartment on my own. It was a trying time for me, but I had to move on.

I was living in Faith, North Carolina. I had a post office box for an address. At the post office, I carried on with the clerks, joking around and kidding. One day I went to the post office and Debbie, one of the postal clerks said, "Joe, you like to have fun and my aunt likes to have fun. I think you two should meet."

Well, I did call Bonnie and talked to her and we dated and later I moved in with her in her house. She came from Washington, DC and bought a house in Rockwell, North Carolina across the street from her sister, Peggy. Bonnie worked at Food Lion in Salisbury, North Carolina. Butch and Sue also worked for Food Lion. Butch is a truck driver and Sue worked in the deli at one of the stores. Bonnie worked at the corporate offices.

I brought my union job with me when I moved in with Bonnie. I thought it was about time to make this job a little easier and to join the 21st century, so at a meeting I requested to procure a computer for the lodge to simplify the bookwork. The members voted to get a computer, so I went to IBM in Raleigh, North Carolina and bought a computer. Then the fun started. I had to learn all about the computer and how to use it. My daughter, Peggy, helped me set up the computer in a bedroom we had made into an office.

While living in the house in Rockwell, North Carolina, We had an addition built onto the house. The addition included a bedroom, bathroom, and a walk-in closet. Bonnie' mother lived with us for a little while; she was in the beginning stage of Alzheimer's. She was a good woman. We used to share a beer together and talk a lot while Bonnie was at work. She would watch television while I was remodeling and working around the house. She used to live with Judy Robinson, Bonnie' sister, in Ponder Cove, Maryland. Judy at the time had a boyfriend named Chuck.

One day she called for me, "Chuck, come in here and see what is on the television." I went to her and said, "Mom, my name is Joe, Chuck used to be Judy's boyfriend in Maryland." She said, "Poor Chuck, Judy did him wrong." She didn't understand that I was trying to correct her to my right name. This happened several times and each time she called me Chuck. Mom's given name was Gladys, so I figured I would call her by the wrong name, she would call me by my right name.

Again, she called me later that day saying, "Chuck, come in here and see this on television." I went into the living room and said, "What is it Nancy?" She said, "Poor Chuck, Judy did him wrong." Well, that didn't work out like I thought it would. I told Bonnie about this when she came home from work. All three of us were sitting in the living room and I left the room to go to the kitchen, when Gladys said, "Bonnie, why is he always calling me Nancy that is a president's wife's name?" Bonnie said, "Well Mom, you started it." Gladys said, "I have never called him Nancy in my life!" My plan didn't work at all.

I formatted spread sheets with formulas and the names of all the members with their information. It was like I was in school again. Oh, but the results were fantastic! When I received my deduction list from payroll in Roanoke, Virginia, all I had to do was change the month name to the new month with any changes, save and print and the work was down to two hours a month instead of two days. Wow! I was really impressed on how far we had progressed into computers. I read the books with the computer and worked on the computer that I became pretty efficient. I could produce letters and mailings and when it came time for elections for the officers of the lodge, I produced the ballots with envelopes so we didn't have to have someone do it for the lodge, thereby saving us money.

I had files upon files on the computer, but still had the paper backup, just in case. When I started out as secretary of the lodge, we had about twelve members. But, in time I had around 60 members I was accounting for. The computer made my life in the union a whole lot easier. I was doing everything on the computer; making spreadsheets, keeping records, typing letters, and much more.

While I was serving as Local Chairman, I used the computer for letters of appeal and official letters needed in my position as officer of the lodge. Just by making copies of these letters, would be evidence of the work involved. My Vice Local Chairman was Rodger Wagner. He was good friend and a dedicated individual. He would help me by documenting the records of the mileage of all the assignments and adjusted the extra board as needed.

The Local Chairman was to enforce the rules of the contract between the Carriers and the union. Of course, there were those who thought I should rule in favor of individuals rather than the lodge. I did not do that. I was to enforce the rules for all concern and not play favorites. But, no matter how I decided, the decision was not going to please everyone. It was a real thankless job.

When I was to start building our house, I had to turn over the Local Chairman work to Rodger, because I did not have the time to be local chairman and build a house at the same time. In my opinion, Rodger was a better Local Chairman than I was.

Chapter Sixteen-Back to the Locals

I was getting very tired of being away from home so much, so I decided to try working the Asheboro Local. The job worked Monday through Saturday, going on duty at 6:00am at High Point, North Carolina and was finished when the work was done or twelve hours, whichever came first. The rail line to Asheboro, North Carolina is twenty six and a half miles long, with about ninety nine road crossings. I had to sound the whistle of the engine at every crossing to warn the public a train was coming. Seems, sounding the whistle is mostly what I did on that job.

One of the trains out of Linwood, North Carolina would bring our cars for the different industries around High Point and for the plants and industries at Asheboro. We would spend several hours switching the cars into the four tracks in the yard, classifying our train (Getting them into station order). There was a road crossing right at the north end of the yard that the train blocked, while we were switching the cars.

Although, this was a small road crossing, there was a lot of traffic going over it, because it was a road that was used by vehicles to get from one side of the railroad tracks to the other side. Highway roads paralleled the yard on both sides. The yard was adjacent to the Thomas Bus factory (They build, naturally, school buses). While we were switching the cars, we blocked the crossing a lot going back and forth with the train. The people in these vehicles got very angry the train was blocking the crossing. There was very little room for the cars to be backed up without causing a major traffic jam.

Knowing what I do about trains having to blocking crossings while the crew was doing their work, I find alternate routes to drive, so I am not delayed at crossings going to my designations. However, these people didn't think of that. I was often told by drivers through a hand gesture that I was the number one engineer (I think that is what that meant), when I was clearing the crossing. Some people actually yelled at me for blocking the crossing saying I was a S.O.B. (I thought that stood for Sweet Old Boy, I could be wrong).

Not only the motorists, but the pedestrians wanting to cross over got agitated. One day, a man was on the off side of train and was climbing through the train, while I was stopped, with a bicycle. I knew this because, when I started to back the train, he jumped out of the way of the cars he was passing through, before they ran over him. When I got to that point, I saw he left the bike to save his life, and I had run over and destroyed the bicycle. He was mad at me for ruining his bike. Go figure.

Another time while I was going back and forth, I was watching two girls walking down the street toward the crossing the train was blocking. It seemed to me that they were still fuzzy from the night before by the way they were weaving, walking down the street. Our two main line tracks were right beside our switching lead. When these two girls got to crossing, they were waiting for us to clear the road, standing in the middle of our number one main track!

When my conductor, Stan Berkshire, told me over the radio to back up I asked him, "Stan, are those girls on the other side of us still in the clear?" He said, "Wait a minute, and I will check." He told me he didn't see the girls. When he came back to my side of the train, he told me, "Joe, you just saved their lives by not moving. They were crossing through the rail cars. One of the girls fell in between the cars and onto ground. The other girl reached in to pull her out of the way of the train." If I had moved the train, when Stan had told me to, I would have run over and killed either one or both of the girls. Why can't people just wait for a few minutes for the train to clear?

Peggy called me and told me Bill Reynolds had been released from prison, after serving ten years of the 18 year sentence. I was really mad at the so-called justice system. I was down on the property and began taking out my frustrations using a machete cutting the underbrush. The next day I told Stan, "If I had a baseball bat, and I ran into Bill Reynolds, I would beat him to death with it!" Stan had two sons that played baseball and he was big into baseball, also. When he showed up for work the next day, without saying a word, he handed me an aluminum baseball bat. I put it in the truck and hoped I would run into Bill one day to rearrange his face. Every curve that I went around in the truck caused the bat to slide and the sound of the bat hitting the wall of the truck reminded me how much anger I felt toward him. I talked to my pastor at Faith Baptist Church in Faith, North Carolina about my anger and the baseball bat. He told me, "Get rid of the baseball bat and leave up to God the vengeance of Bill Reynolds." I did exactly that.

The day was very long on the Asheboro Local. Not so much because of the work, but the speed limit of tracks prevented us from getting over the road quicker. But, there was a lot of work on the job, also. At the end of the line in Asheboro, we switched out Georgia Pacific. The industry only held four cars to be unloaded. We usually switched them out at the end of the day before we got off duty, and again the first thing in the next morning when we came back to work.

We called the taxi cab company to meet us where we were going to stop the train for the night, so they could take us back to High Point where went off duty, got into our personal vehicles, and went home. Stan and I shared a ride going to and from work. When we got off duty at High Point, North Carolina, we usually got a six pack for the ride home. Stan was very interesting character. We would have long conversations about the different kinds of beer, life, marriage, and everything else. He was funny and I liked him a lot.

I tried to watch him closely, so he wouldn't take any unnecessary chances with his life, while working around the engines and rail cars. It was against the rules to kick the drawbar of the rail car to adjust its position to couple to the train. Stan had a bad habit of doing just that, just before the engine was going to make contact with car.

There are cases documented where a man was attempting to kick the drawbar with his foot, missed the drawbar, and had his foot cut off when the cars were coupled together. There were cases where men had been coupled up in between two cars. They would live until the cars were separated, then they would fall dead. Not pleasant to see those happen.

When I saw he was going to do this, I tried to stop the engine before making contact with the car. I would yell at him not to do that for he might get hurt of fired (Suspended from service) for violating the rules. I was proud that I was making him think about it to the extent, that at least he was looking around to see if anyone was watching before he did it.

Now more than ever, the officials would have rule checks to see if the crews were working by the rules. There sure were a lot of them. It was pretty easy to find rule violations on a train crew, if they were watched for any length of time. It could be as simple as not bending over to throw a switch properly or a major infraction. As for the engineers, it could be not wearing safety glasses to speeding and everything in between.

Anytime a train derailed, the first thing the company did was to pull the tapes off of the engines. This was a recording device like the black box on airplanes. They resembled eight track tapes that measured the location, speed, throttle position, among other things of what the engines were doing. The track department would never take responsibility for the derailment unless the train crews were exonerated first. That seemed the opinion of the trainmasters as well. The Road Forman and Trainmasters were the supervisors of the engineers and train crews, respectively.

One derailment I had was when I was going over a track portion that had extensive work performed on it. The heat had a dramatic effect on the rails. The rail would expand in the heat, causing it to buckle out of alignment. The span in between the rails was 56-57 ½ inches to accommodate the wheels of the train. If the span was any greater than that, the train wheels fell on the ground. This part of the track was riding rougher than usual this day. When the engines went over this section of track, they swayed from one side to the other, but when the rail cars came over it, they starting turning over. We derailed about five cars, with two of them lying on their side.

The highway beside the track was filled with onlookers that observed the train derailing and the aftermath. The derailment was at a crossing and had anyone been there waiting for the train to pass, they would have had a one hundred and thirty ton rail car on top of their vehicle crushing it and anyone inside. Fortunately, there was no one there.

They pulled the tapes off of the engines, as always, and found that we were not speeding. The track department tried to get out of it, but they had to accept the responsibility of that derailment. It wasn't for lack of trying to pin it on me, although they tried.

Another time, we were trying to get back into High Point, North Carolina from Asheboro before the hours of service law got us (We could not work over twelve hours). I was getting the speed of the train down to ten MPH to enter the yard limits. I was looking at the road crossing ahead and it just didn't look right. The rails looked like they had been spread out over the 57 ½ inches. I thought if, while I was reducing my speed, I could keep the slack out of the rail cars, we would go over this part of track safely. I had all the slack out of the train and the engines went over the bad rail okay, but the more the train got on that part of the track, the slower we became. About seven of the rail cars derailed, falling into the excessive gap. The derailed cars stayed upright, but at least the cars didn't turn over.

What had happened, we found out, was that a bulldozer had run over the crossing, and in doing so, had spread the rails. We went home that night without doing anything else, but the next day, we assisted the track gang in the re-railing of the cars. The re-railing of the cars took a few hours, so we were behind with our work when we were finished.

After we switched our train and were ready to go, we backed out of the yard, and stopped at a diner for lunch. After lunch, we would proceed down the road, stopping at our spots to work the industries. Yet again, on this job, I encountered people driving to the railroad tracks without looking for train traffic. One such incident was in Archdale, North Carolina. A man drove into the small airport where the entrance to the airport is also the exit. When he was coming out of the airport, he did not look for a train until the last moment, stopping just short of the first rail, which did not clear the width of the engine. I could not stop the train quickly enough and the impact of the collision took off the bumper of his car. I saw him slam his fists down on the steering wheel in frustration for being hit by the train.

The very next week, we were traveling west from Asheboro, North Carolina to High Point, North Carolina, when a woman driving a car crossed in front of the train without stopping. We hit the car at twenty five miles per hour and send the car tumbling upside down into the bamboo that was growing pretty high by the scrap metal place we were going to stop at to switch. She was okay, but I can't say the same thing about her car, that was destroyed.

We were going east toward Asheboro, North Carolina the next day and as we approached this crossing, we noticed that a lot of the bamboo was cut down for better visibility of the road traffic and the claim agent for the railroad was taking pictures of the scene of the collision with the car the day before. The cutting down of the bamboo had nothing to do with the visibility of the train from the day before. I guess this was hindsight or the railroad was trying to cover their butt.

Most railroad people having a hearing loss to some degree. I guess mine came from being too close to the whistle that was sounded at every crossing by me. I became deaf in my left ear, between high frequency and speech. What someone says to me is not exactly what I hear. To give you an example of that, Bonnie and I were riding in my new Ford 250, and I was still smelling the new truck smell, when I thought she said, "Terry bought a 250 Ford."

I replied, "Terri?"

Bonnie: "Yes, my niece Terri."

Joe: "Terri bought a truck?"

Bonnie: "Truck?"

Joe: "You just said that Terri bought a 250 Ford."

Bonnie: "No, I said she bowled a 254"

We were having two different conversations. I tried to find humor in my loss of hearing, and sometimes it is all too easy to misinterpret what I think I heard. The loss of hearing has been replaced by a constant humming or buzzing sound. This is called Tinnitus. I try to have a constant sound around me to mask the ringing in my ear. When there is no sound around me, the ringing gets very loud. The ringing in my ears sometimes brings me to tears. I feel like yelling out, "Somebody answer that phone."

I was helping Tom build a house in a sub-division near Faith, Carolina. At the end of the housing development was a lot of land for sell that had acreage. I was not thinking about buying any land to build a house, but that property sure did look good. It was three acres of land that sloped down to a creek running through the middle of the property. I always like having a basement in a house and this land called for a house with a basement.

Bonnie and talked it over and we decided to buy that land. It was so thick with trees and growth that it was hard to get through all the land. Bonnie and I spent four hours one Sunday afternoon just trying to mark the surrounding lines of the land. We were not going to build for a while, so we had time to clean up the land. My daughter, Peggy and her husband George helped me a great deal cleaning the underbrush and cutting down dead trees. It was a constant work in progress. After work,

I would go to the property and just sit on the ground and watch the wind go through the trees, while thinking about building the house.

I went to the Sanford Local that went on duty in Greensboro, North Carolina. This job also worked six days a week, but I was home only every other day. The job went to Sanford, North Carolina on Mondays, Wednesdays, and Fridays, and returned to Greensboro, North Carolina on Tuesdays Thursdays and Saturdays. We worked twelve hours nearly every day. But this was the job I needed to get some money saved up, so we could start building our house.

There were three feed mills that we switched in Bonlee, North Carolina. The railroad hauled about 25,000 tons of grain a week to be made into chicken feed to supply the chicken houses all around the area. The finished product was put into large trucks and delivered to the chicken houses. From chicken egg to grocery shelf is only eleven weeks. Now, you would think that the people that worked at these industries with railroad sidings would be aware of trains or engines going over their crossings. But, that does not matter, people do not like waiting for trains.

We were leaving Bonlee, North Carolina going back to Greensboro, North Carolina one day and as we approached a crossing at one of the mills, we saw an 18 wheeler come across the crossing in front of us. He stopped at the stop sign for the highway, but was stopped on the railroad. When he saw the train coming, he had to pull out onto the highway in front of a car to clear the crossing before we hit him. I didn't think he was going to clear me in time, so I was trying to stop the train. He pulled out into the road and hugging the shoulder of the road to avoid being hit by the car while the rear of his trailer was dropping off the road when he cleared the crossing. All of that could have been avoided if he would have stopped at the crossing and look for the train before going over the crossing. Oh well!

After regaining speed, we continued on toward Greensboro. We came through Liberty, North Carolina, going around a curve to the crossing at Allen's Hatchery. I was sounded the whistle to the crossing and to our horror a truck was going over the crossing without stopping. I saw him looking for the train when he was on the crossing, a little late then! I knew we were going to hit the truck. He punched the accelerator to clear the crossing, even leaned forward in the seat to clear the rail himself.

We hit him at thirty miles an hour at 5:10pm, separated the tractor from the trailer, knocking the tractor into eleven other vehicles, belonging to employees who worked there. The impact of the engine, destroying the trailer, pushed the grab irons up against the front door, so we could not even go out the front door. The trailer was destroyed, along with 24,000 eggs in their special crates going to incubation. The eggs and the special crates that held them were more expensive than the truck-trailer rig itself.

The collision with the egg truck turned the black and white engine into a yellow and white engine. The fire department had to wash the engine windshield with the fire hose, before the egg yolk dried. A female reporter for the Greensboro News and Record came to the collision to write about the collision for the newspaper.

In the article of the newspaper the next day, a caption over the picture of the collision read, "X-Large Mess." Some of the excerpts from the article were, "There were yards of yoke.", "There was a breakfast aroma everywhere.", and "The local yokels came out to see the collision." The more I read, the madder I got, and I felt I had to right the wrong. I called the newspaper to chastise them for making light of this potentially ghastly collision. Naturally, I could not reach a human, just a metallic voice, so I was forced to write a letter. My letter was published a day after the mayor of Liberty had his published, chastising the paper for referring to his citizens as "Local Yokels."

What I wrote was this, "You had a lot of fun with this train- egg truck collision the other day. You must have thought it was amusing, but we train crew members take it as serious. The truck driver could have lost his life, but he just lost his job.

If you think that was funny, you'll die laughing at this. I was driving a train at night out of Burlington, North Carolina going uphill at 20 MPH. I saw what I thought was a box on the rail, but when I got closer, I saw it was a man sitting on the rail. When I sounded the whistle for him to get off the track, he just fell forward. When I hit and killed him with the train, I smelled alcohol and blood.

I was coming out of Mebane, North Carolina at 49 MPH and I saw a car stalled on the tracks. The driver did not try to get out of the car nor get his car off of the tracks. I hit him with the train and he died on the way to the hospital. His daughter was on a school bus behind him and she had witnessed her father being killed by the train.

I was coming around a curve in Thomasville, North Carolina at 50 MPH. A Volkswagen was reported to race its engine to beat me to the crossing. I hit the vehicle in the passenger side of the car, knocking the car into a signal mast, knocking it down. The train stopped about a mile down the track, and when the train crew members went back to the collision, they found a three year old girl dead in the passenger seat.

Instead of being a source of entertainment, we have the Sunday comics for that, you could be a source of education to teach people to Look, Listen, and Live®."

The news media do not allow the facts of an incident to get in the way of their reporting. Of course, I didn't hear anything back from the newspaper. The newspapers seem satisfied in reporting deaths and injuries, rather than try to do anything to help stop them. There was an eye witness to this train-truck collision. He was at the intersection across the road from Allen's, and he saw the whole scene unfold, and the claim agent said he was a good witness. If it wasn't for testimony of that witness, people would believe that I would chase vehicles down in an open field to hit them with the train.

We were heading for Sanford, North Carolina one day and as we were rounded a curve, I saw something too close to the track. As we got closer, I saw that it was an 18 wheeler that had come off the highway bridge and crashed onto the railroad. The driver of the truck was walking toward us on the tracks waving for us to stop. I was sounded the whistle and yelling at him for him to get off the tracks. It is pretty bad to hit vehicles with the train at crossings, but this collision occurred where there was no road crossing. The driver of the truck had swerved to avoid hitting a tractor mowing grass. As he tried to swerve back in his lane, the trailer of the truck hit the tractor, causing the big truck to run off the road and down the embankment crashing onto the railroad tracks. He had a truck accident and then the truck was hit by a train.

Another job that worked on that Sanford branch was the E-12, which worked the industries the Sanford Local did not switch. The conductor was Ernie Williams and the brakeman was Bill Torbush. I had worked with Bill going to Roanoke and other jobs. I really enjoyed working with them because they were very good railroad men. I made a suggestion one day to the trainmaster about our operations and using "common sense" in our work. He said, "We are not going to allow common sense interfere with the way we do business." Well, there you go. Another reason for the title of this book!

I worked that job when I could, because they worked less hours. I was going to need some spare time on my side to build our house. I talked to Tom Graham about him building the house with me, and he said he would. I was going to contract the house and Tom and I would accept bids from the other craftsmen, like plumbers, electricians, brick masons, and roofers. Tom's input and thoughts on the planning and building of the house would be invaluable.

We broke ground in May of 2000, when we had a bulldozer dig the basement. I was right about the land calling for a basement, if not a basement, we would have had a ten foot high crawl space. The front and side walls could resist 200 MPH winds and was an R-50 rating. The beams throughout the structure could accommodate large areas without supporting beams or walls.

My brother, Len, worked third shift at Freightliner©. When Len got off of work on the night shift, he helped Tom build the house until I came home after work. Tom and I usually worked until dark thirty, and then we would drink beer discussing the next days' agenda. I remember working to 1130pm one night and had to get up the next morning at 430am to go to work on the railroad. It was a taxing adventure, both mentally and physically.

On one our trips back to Greensboro, North Carolina on E-12, we were approaching a crossing in Vandalia, North Carolina. There was a school bus stopped clear of the railroad tracks at a crossing with lights and gates. As we approached the crossing at 25 MPH about 1200 feet from the crossing, the lights and bells at the crossing were activated. To our amazement, the school bus driver took that opportunity to cross the tracks. There was a backup of cars at the stop sign entering the highway, so the bus stopped behind the cars in the middle of the tracks. When I saw the bus stopped in the tracks, I put the train into emergency so hard that I jammed my hand into my wrist, but I was going to do anything I could to stop before hitting a school bus.

As luck would have it, a car moved out into the intersection that allowed the bus to move clear of rails as we came over the crossing and missed the school bus by three feet. It was a very unnerving experience to see the children's faces on the school bus, wondering if I was going to hit them. We reported the incident to the dispatcher, and gave him the school bus number. Usually the school will fire the driver, thank goodness! Every time I was approaching a crossing and I saw a school bus coming to the same crossing, the hair on the back of my neck stood up and I got goose bumps on my arm. I was praying that the school bus would stop at the crossing as required by the law.

I was the engineer on E-12 when I had two other collisions with trucks. We were heading back to Greensboro, North Carolina and approaching a crossing just west of Allen's Hatchery. I saw a truck come out of an industry and I saw the driver looking down at a clipboard, instead of looking for our train. He looked up too late; we hit him at 25 MPH and knocked the truck out from under him. He sustained a broken leg so bad that the doctors had to put pins in his leg to hold his leg together. The driver was fortunate not to have been run over by the engine or his own truck.

The other truck, another 18 wheeler, cut through a parking lot in Pleasant Garden, North Carolina and went over the tracks without stopping. He looked for the train when he was on the rail crossing. He had tried to accelerate over the crossing without being hit. The train clipped the rear of the trailer knocking it into a fence. The engine ripped off his hydraulic lift on the rear of the trailer. Pleasant Garden Road runs parallel with the railroad tracks for several miles. While in the Highway Patrol car, the truck driver admitted that he saw the train, for he followed alongside the train for miles on the road.

All the other collisions I had with vehicles, I completed my duty until the end of the day. But, this time I asked for a relief. I was just so sick and tired of hitting vehicles with the train. I did not realize how much stress the collisions were putting on me. Every crossing I came to, I was envisioning a half of a vehicle coming out from the other side. I was really getting nervous at each and every crossing.

The Road Foreman of Engines wanted to talk to me in his car at this collision when I asked for a relief. When I got into the car with him he said, "Are you going to be alright?" I said, "Yes, I will make it." Then he said. "Consider this as a counseling session." I was flabbergasted. I wanted to say so bad, "If you kiss me on the cheek, I will have considered us having sex!" That was some counseling session!

The trainmaster called me on the way home after I got into my own personal vehicle. He wanted to know if I was going to be at work the next day. I was trying to gather my thoughts, and not think about railroading for a while. I started to cry and I asked him if I could be put into the Operation Lifesaver® program, for I wanted to do anything I could to stop these meaningless collisions from happening. He said he would see what he could do.

During this time, we were building our house. After working on the house until quitting time, we spent time drinking beer sitting on buckets of sheetrock filler, and planning the next phase of building. We usually called a restaurant by cell phone to order supper. When my grandson, Drew, was with us, we were reinforcing his table manners, like asking permission to get up from the table and taking his dirty dish to the kitchen. I realized he was learning, when we were sitting around on buckets and the floor of the unfinished house eating pizza. When Drew was through eating, he asked, "May I get up from the floor?"

Drew was a true boy. When we went down to the property just after Jason had dug the basement, there was a big pile of red dirt. I had no longer shut the door of the truck, when I saw Drew on top of the red clay sliding down the mound of dirt. He had red dirt all over him, in his shorts and socks. I yelled out to him, "You're staying clean, aren't you son?" He said, "Yes Sir!"

Again, I was tired of being on the road all the time, so I made a move to work a yard engine at Linwood, North Carolina. I told Ernie Williams and Bill Torbush, "I love working with you guys, but I am going to work a job a little closer to home." Bill Torbush had just got married and I had attended and video tapped his wedding. Nine days after I had left the job and just thirty days after his wedding, Bill was killed in a railroad accident.

Ernie and Bill had left their train clear of a crossing to go switch a mill at Bonlee, North Carolina. When they were through switching, they headed back to get the rest of the train at the crossing. There was a loss of communication on the radio between Bill and the engineer as they approached the train. As Bill went out of the engine door, the engines coupled to the 13,000 freight train crushing Bill to death. The impact was so hard that the lead car was derailed. The derailed car weighed 130 tons. When I heard about Bill's death, I cried for a long time. Railroad workers become close friends, and when one dies or gets killed, it is like a member of your family that has died. We had known each other and worked together for over thirty years. Railroading has always been a dangerous profession, but these fatalities could be avoided if people would just ask, "What if?" Thinking about what could happen could save their lives.

Chapter Seventeen Operation Lifesaver®

I was sent to Raleigh, North Carolina to attend an Operation Lifesaver® class in July of 2002. At the end of the class, I had to make a ten minute presentation about Operation Lifesaver®, using the flip charts to illustrate the hazards and dangers around the railroad tracks. I was a little nervous doing my first presentation in front of people. I had to make a presentation with a mentor within a certain time frame to fully qualify as a presenter. My mentor was Jim Valley. He had been a presenter for years.

Jim had setup presentations to be given to 276 Davidson County school bus drivers and he wanted me to go with him and give the presentations to get my "feet wet." Jim and I went to lunch that day with the assistant to the transportation department of school buses. During our conversation over lunch, I told her about the tragic deaths that led me to become a presenter. She replied, "Just get over it!" Oh wow, I should have thought of that. That sounds so simple, but I know it is not that easy. So, that is how I got started into the business of saving lives around the railroad tracks.

I wanted to give as many presentations as I could, to anyone who would listen to me, and teach them how to save their lives around the tracks. I gave about 34 presentations from August until the end of the year. I presented to logging truck drivers, civic and church groups, driver education classes, school events, kindergarten classes, truck driving schools, and anyone else that would have me come in and speak to them.

North Carolina Operation Lifesaver® (www.ncol.org) has quarterly meetings to see how they are doing, reviewing statistics, and planning events. The quarterly meeting held in December is the awards banquet. Vivian Bridges, the State Coordinator, after lunch, gives out awards to the outstanding presenters. That year I received the "Rookie of the Year", for giving more presentations than any other new presenter.

What I did was, whenever we had to stop the train for any reason near the industries that we worked, I would go into the office and ask them if they would allow me to give a presentation about railroad safety. Most of the people would set up a time and date I could come in and do the presentation. I was becoming more and more confident giving the presentations. It is not the easiest thing to do, standing in front of strangers talking.

I started out by giving the presentations at the industries that I had collisions with vehicles or near misses with vehicles. The railroad called the near hits as near misses. A lot of the industries had just one way into the facility and one way back out, over the railroad tracks. At the start of one of my presentations at such a place, I asked the audience, "How many of you had to cross railroad tracks to get to work today?" About half of the people raised their hands. I said, "The rest of you people must have come in by helicopter!" If they were there, they had to cross the tracks to be there. That shows how much people pay attention to the railroad tracks.

Farmers Day is held in China Grove, North Carolina every year in July and it is a very fair-like, festive occasion. They have many vendors providing food and crafts displays. Toward the end of the evening, they have a street dance and fireworks. My friends, Cecelia and Joey Patterson live just one house off of Main Street and all the festivities. The walking up and down the street by the vendors, CeCe refers to as "The China Grove Five Hundred." While walking the "Five Hundred", I stopped by one of the exhibits that were giving people free blood pressure checks. My blood pressure was 176 over 106, my goodness; I was a heart attack waiting for a happening.

I was a little overweight, but I could not understand why my blood pressure was so high. I went to my doctor, Gary Fink, and after several months and visits, the medicine had lowered my blood pressure to more respectful levels. He also recommended for me to see a psychiatrist to get me on a "High Anxiety" pill, politically correct for an anti depressant. Seems like my nerves were shot, perhaps because of the pain I was feeling for Peggy. I told Linda that I wanted to hunt Bill Reynolds down and kill him. But no, it was more than that I figured, for every time I did a presentation, I was getting more and more emotional during the presentation. I was re-living every collision that I had with those vehicles and those memories of those people killed by the train as I did the presentations.

I was giving a presentation to a driver education class at South Rowan High School showing the class a picture of a train that had a destroyed car on the front of it. The vehicle was really crushed by the train. Upon seeing this picture, one student blurted out coldly, "What kind of car is it?" After the presentation, I had to call my psychiatrist for another session. Linda was trying to console me saying, "Joe, you did not kill these people, the train did." But, I told her, "Linda, I have to live with the emotion of these deaths by the train, the train has no emotion."

The next month when I gave another presentation at the same high school, if anyone asked that question again, I had an answer for them. "This is not a car, it's a coffin. Was there anything I could do to stop the train quicker? Oh God, were there any children in the car? Did they leave home that day and tell their loved ones, 'I love you very much, but I'll never see you again, because I am going to be killed by a train?'" That is what I think about, not what kind of car it is.

I started walking three to five miles almost every day and within a year or so, I lost fifty pounds, lowered my blood pressure, quit drinking, and I felt the best I had felt for years. My eyes filled up with tears now; instead of having tears run down my cheek during the presentation like before I was on the "High Anxiety" pill. The message had to given, even if it did hurt me emotionally. I was obsessed to give as many presentations as I could, not for the recognition or awards, but for the sake of saving lives of those people who cross the railroad tracks at one time or another.

I was going to retire in 2004, because I would be sixty years old with over thirty years service, the qualifying criteria. I took my vacation at the end of December of 2003, so I knew I would be off for Christmas and the quarterly meeting of North Carolina Operation Lifesaver® held in Cary, North Carolina. Bonnie did not want to make the trip, so my daughter, Peggy, went with me to the banquet. I found out later that Vivian Bridges had talked to Peggy to get me there to attend the meeting. The reason, I found out, was that I received three awards that day; "Volunteer of the Year", "Presenter of the Year", and the "Directors Award." The only award I didn't win was the "Media Award", for which I did not qualify. I was really surprised!

I made a website for myself with Operation Lifesaver® as the main theme throughout all the pages, (www.thetrainman.biz). I tried to save people's lives around the railroad tracks all over the world. The United States is not the only country that has a problem with fatalities with the train. Believe it not, I decided to go to Rowan-Cabarrus Community College after I retired, to make my website better and take other computer classes as well as the mandatory classes. I was the oldest student in my classes, and older than the professors. I always figured that I am never too old to learn, for I have always had a thirst for knowledge.

What I had learned by reading computer books helped me in making straight "A's" in my courses. Of course I had to apply myself to study to make good grades. The students that came out of high school and into college brought high school mentality with them to college. My first class was at 8:00am and went on to 8:50am. Some students came in as late as 8:30 to attend class. If I were the teacher, I would have sent them away and locked the door. Some were always late, like the class will wait for me to start. Cell phones were always ringing disturbing the rest of the class, even though the rules of the campus prohibited that sort of thing. Hello people? This is a place of learning, not a social event.

I formatted my e-mail address on my website so people could get in touch with me. When I gave the presentations, I encouraged the audience to send me a message. When I didn't receive any e-mails from anyone, I was wondering if I formatted the address correctly. I had a couple of e-mail addresses, so I e-mail myself to see if the system was working. When I received the e- mail, I e-mailed back to me replying that I had received it.

You see, it is alright to talk to yourself, and is okay to answer yourself. But, when you answer, "What did you say?" that's when it's all over. I told everyone just to e-mail me and tell me that my jokes stink. That way I would know they were listening to me and they would never go over the tracks without thinking about me. If they thought about me, then they would think about the train and I know that I would have saved their lives.

I started getting e-mails from my presentations then, and I would always answer them. I had one student to e-mail me and said, "Thank you Mr. Harris for taking the time to give us your presentation, it was awesome! Your jokes stink (You told me to tell you that).I understand why you use your humor to open up our mind, it is so you can give us information on how to save our life around the railroad tracks." This young man saw right through my plan. That is exactly how I tried to get their attention is with silly jokes like, "You know that a train has been by here, because the train has left its tracks."

While I was going to college, Peggy was attending Catawba College, while working full time for Rowan County. That is difficult. I couldn't do that, but I admire people who do, for they are special, dedicated people. She graduated with honors in 2006, and I was so proud of her accomplishments. The graduation was fifteen years late, because of her having to drop out of Western Carolina for personal reasons. She was determined, I'll give her that.

In her last year of college, she took an environment course, which included turning my backyard into a registered National Wildlife Federation Habitat. The presentation that she gave on my habitat was graded. She graduated with a 3.96 GPA, so I think she did well on it. We feed the numerous birds and squirrels and have wildlife on the property that includes; ducks, raccoons, hawks, owls, beavers, and deer. In the creek and self-made pond, we have fish and frogs.

While I was attending college, I was still finding time to give Operation Lifesaver® presentations. I was presenting to the driver's education classes in all the high schools in Alamance County. The trip to Burlington, North Carolina was 150 miles round trip, so I try to be at two schools in one day while I was there.

The driver education students were fourteen and fifteen years old and some of them did not take the classes or my presentation serious. In one class while I was speaking, four girls were working on their papers, either writing or reading. I went up to their table tapping on the table saying, "I did not bring my homework with me, so you may put yours away." I demanded attention, for I told them, "The same attention you give me today is the same attention you give the train coming down the railroad tracks." One student was texting on their phone, while I was speaking. The instructor knew of my emotional status for he had heard the presentation numerous times before. Because of this inattention, the student was kicked out of class by the instructor. I have no fear in pointing out the students for not listening to me, because they have to realize the responsibility of driving a vehicle and the results of a collision with a train.

I started out my presentation asking, "Has anyone ever heard about Operation Lifesaver®?" One student raised his hand. I asked, "Great son, what is about?" He said, "I don't know, I just heard about it." It is amazing to me the number of people who have never heard about Operation Lifesaver®. Therefore; I had to change my question to, "Does anyone know what Operation Lifesaver® is about?" I was talking to one student at Graham High School before one class started, and he told me he remembered me from the month before. I asked him, "Did you fail the class and have to take it over?" He said, "No, I just missed a couple of days, so I had to make them up." I said, "Well, you will know what Operation Lifesaver® is when I ask you." When I asked him about it though, he said, "You want us to donate our organs when we are killed in an accident." I said, "I see why you are repeated this class now."

The instructors of the driver education classes also have police officers or Highway Patrol officers come to the class to speak to the students. There is a person to speak to them about being an organ donor so that others can live through organ transplants. I told the class, "I want you to keep all of your organs and I hope you live a long life. I want to save your life, before it gets to the point of donating your organs. I do not want them."

At one point giving presentations, I was spending $200 to $300 a month for fuel for my vehicles driving all over the state of North Carolina. The presentations were free, but my expenses were my own. I was giving out pamphlets and key chains to everyone and something for the instructors for my appreciation for allowing me to talk to their students.

I also went to Greensboro, North Carolina to Greensboro Day School where Craig Head had his "Heads up Driving School." Mr. Head really appreciated me giving the presentations to his class. When I attended his December classes, he gave me a Christmas gift. They were fuel cards so I could fill up my truck with fuel. I tried to tell him that I didn't want him to be obligated to get fuel for me, but he insisted.

He was really grateful for me to teach his kids about the safety around the railroad tracks. He told me once, "There is a lot of difference in the students driving to the railroad tracks that heard your stories, as opposed to those of them that have not sat in on your presentation." He had felt my pain and really did thank me for sharing my stories with his classes.

I took my grandson, Drew, with me to one of Mr. Head's driver education class. Drew, six years old at the time, was watching the video intently, although he had been with me a number of times before, and had seen the video many times. While everyone was watching the film, Drew got up off of the floor where he was sitting, walked up to a couple of girls, said something to them, and then went back to sit down. After the presentation was over, I asked Drew what he did. He said, "Those girls were talking, so I told them, "He is trying to save your lives, you need to pay attention." Those fourteen year old girls got put down by a six year old! Drew being with me so many times on my trips, knew more about Operation Lifesaver® than the people I was teaching.

Vivian called one day and asked me if I was able to go to Duke Energy in Charlotte, North Carolina to give about 200 people an Operation Lifesaver® Presentation. I said, "Sure, I will." She told me, "There will be vice-presidents on down in attendance, so dress nicely, but give your message from the heart." I got dress up in a suit and tie, which was rare for me as everyday apparel and I went to Charlotte on the assigned day.

I was in a large conference room with about 200 people, large TV screen, and a microphone on my lapel, three remote controls for the computer devices and equipment, and ready to start. I was a high-tech redneck. I looked over the audience and the first thing I said was, "Vivian told me to dress nicely for this event, but give my presentation from the heart, but I am the only sucker here dressed in a suit and tie!" I told the large group of people that it does not matter what you wear, or who you are, when you are hit by the train, you are going to be equally as dead. I received ten e-mails from people at that presentation saying they were going to pass that information on to their children. That is so rewarding for people to take the time to write about what they had learned, and that they were going to teach others.

In a small article in the Salisbury Post, I read about a woman killed by Amtrak in Mebane, North Carolina. I had tears in my eye when I finished reading, because I felt if I had talked to more people in Alamance County about Operation Lifesaver®, she would not have been killed. I gave presentations to the fire departments around that area and I found out the whole story about that collision.

She was in her car sitting at a stop light on the tracks. When Amtrak was approaching, causing the railroad gates to come down, she tried to maneuver her car off of the tracks. It was too little, too late; Amtrak hit her at about 70 MPH. The collision threw her body 85 feet from the impact. The rescue squad people told me they found a toe on one side of the tracks, and her head was on the other side. An arm was on one side of the tracks and an eyeball was on the other side. It was very gruesome, but very real.

When I told another driver education class in Greensboro, North Carolina about this tragic death, several students started laughing! This angered me and I told them, "Maybe you wouldn't think that was so funny if it was your mother, grandmother, or someone you love?" I sure didn't think it was funny. People watch TV and see these horrific collisions and the people involved survive, or they think that it won't happen to them. But, that is only on television, surviving being hit by a train is nothing short of a miracle.

The facts are, every two hours, there is going to be a collision with a train and a motor vehicle. Fifty percent of these collisions occur at crossings with active warning devices, such as lights and gates. Twenty-one percent of these collisions occur, when the vehicle runs into the side of the train. Most people are killed or injured within twenty five miles of their home. Most years, more people are killed by trains in a year than those people killed in airline crashes. (These statistics vary little year by year). Six hundred to seven hundred people are killed each year trying to beat the train, or by trespassing on the railroad right of way. These are all preventable, for all you have to do is stay off the tracks.

It is not like the news reports that say the trains chase people down in an open field to kill them. It just doesn't work that way. The news people have reported that, "The conductor of the train was blowing his whistle to warn the people to get off of the tracks.", or "The conductor was trying to stop the train." Never once in my thirty years of operating the train, has my conductor been sitting on my lap, sounding the whistle of the train or trying to apply the air brakes to the train.

When I am following a vehicle in my truck approaching the railroad tracks, I always look at the person ahead of me in their car to see if they turn their heads to look for the train. It is scary to see that ninety percent of the people driving do not look for the train, until they are on the tracks. I compare that with looking down the barrel of a gun, then pulling the trigger to see if the gun is loaded.

I went to several truck driving schools to teach the students about Operation Lifesaver®. The last four vehicles I hit with the train were professional truck drivers. The railroad closed the dormitory at Linwood North Carolina, and Carolina Driving Institute established a truck driving school in its place. I went by the school several times and noticed there were more and more vehicles parked there, so I decided to stop in there one day to see if I could give the students a presentation. The director of the school is Dennis Zaferatos.

I talked to Dennis for a while and he said, "Sure, I want you to come in and talk to my students." Every month or so when they had a new class enrolled, I would go and give another presentation to the new students. Some of the students would be filling out their log books while I was speaking and I would have to tell them, "You can put all your books away and pay attention to me, for the same attention you pay to me is the same attention you give the train, and I don't you to be killed by the train."

When I decided to come out of retirement and go back to work, I asked Dennis if I could enroll in his class to become a truck driver. He asked me, like he does all his students, "Are you sure you want to do this?" I said I did, and I went that day to start class. The whole staff at the school was very nice and very helpful. The instructors were professional truck drivers. After a month, I had all my hours in classroom, driving, and observing, and I was ready to test out or graduate from truck driving school. I passed with flying colors, so to speak and I was hired by U.S.Xpress, Inc, Enterprises.

My trainer was Ronnie Lowe for six weeks until I was ready to drive on my own. I upgraded to first seat driver in Oklahoma City, Oklahoma. In the first seven months driving a truck, I went into 46 out of the lower 48 states. I have seen countless number of accidents involving trucks as well as cars. People are not willing to give their full attention to driving. I see them talking on the cell phone, texting, eating, reading books, and using laptop computers while driving. Some states are requiring hands free phones. That is not the problem; it is the mind that is off of the driving, not the hands. If we have our attention on other than driving, there will more accidents.

To solidify this point, a woman was talking on a phone in her car following a dump truck on Interstate 40 in Greensboro, North Carolina. When the dump truck went off of the road and into the construction zone, she followed the truck right in there with him. Realizing her error, she stopped and had to back out into the interstate. How much attention do people have on driving, when doing all these other things? My answer is zero. But, I will have to address those issues in my next book, "Hell of a Way to Drive a Truck"

While attending college, in my first year English class, I had to write a personal essay. I chose to write about, "How I got into Operation Lifesaver®" I had to have a closing paragraph in my personal essay. My closing paragraph was like this:

"I have received numerous awards for giving Operation Lifesaver® presentations. All those awards and six dollars will let you purchase a cheeseburger at a fast food restaurant. The awards are collecting dust in a bookcase. But, if I can save one life through my presentations, prevent one collision, or prevent one train crew member from going through the emotional distress that I have endured for years, all of my efforts will be worth it.

In conclusion, be cautious going to the railroad tracks, always expect a train, and "In case of a tie, you lose!" I hope this book has been entertaining as well as informative. If you follow the guidelines of Operation Lifesaver®, they will save your life. As one student told me, "Operation Lifesaver® is about an operation that saves lives." Well, he was right, but he was pulling that answer out his magic hat.

References

1990s, Railroads of the. *HowStuffWorks.com*. Publications International, Ltd. April 18, 2008. <http://history.howstuffworks.com/american-history/1990s-railroads.htm> (accessed May 04, 2009).

Brain, Marshall. *HowStuffWorks.com*. How Diesel Engines Work. April 01, 2000. <http://auto.howstuffworks.com/diesel.htm (accessed May 04, 2009).

Ehrenreich, Thomas. *Catskill Archive*. 2001. http://www.railroadextra.com (accessed April 15, 2009).

Ehrenreich, Thomas, B.W. Allen, and F.W. Smoter. *www.catskillarchive.com*. http://www.catskillarchive.com/rrextra/glossry1.Html (accessed April 15, 2009).

Hubbard, Freeman H. *Railroad Terms and Glossary* . Railroad Avenue, 1945.

Railroads, Modern Decline of. *HowStuffWorks.com*. Publications International, Ltd. April 18, 2008. <http://history.howstuffworks.com/american-history/decline-of-railroads.htm> (accessed May 04, 2009).

Railroads, Post-war. *HowStuffWorks.com*. Publications International, Ltd. April 17, 2008. <http://history.howstuffworks.com/american-history/post-war-railroads.htm> (accessed May 04, 2009).

Yebba, Anthony R. *USS Fremont* XE "USS Fremont" . http://www.ussfremont.org/frewin.html (accessed April 1, 2008).

Railroad Terms and Glossary

This Glossary of Railroad Lingo is from: Railroad Avenue, by Freeman H. Hubbard, 1945 * Designates Contributed by BW Allen. BNSF Locomotive Engineer # Designates Contributed by FW Smoter. Web Master Johnstown Flood Page (Ehrenreich, Catskill Archive 2001) (Ehrenreich, Allen and Smoter, www.catskillarchive.com n.d.)

AGE—Seniority, length of service

AIR MONKEY—Air-brake repairman

* ALL DARKIE, NO SPARKY—(Hi-Ball on a roll by)

ALLEY—Clear track in railroad yard

ANCHOR THEM—Set hand brakes on still cars; the opposite is release anchors

ARMSTRONG—Old-style equipment operated by muscular effort, such as hand-brakes, some turntables, engines without automatic stokers, etc.

ARTIST—Man who is particularly adept, usually with prefix such as brake, pin, speed, etc.

ASHCAT—Locomotive fireman

BACK TO THE FARM— Lay off on account of slack business. When a man is discharged he is given six months twice a year

BAD ORDER— Crippled car or locomotive, often called cripple. Must be marked at night by a blue light when men are working around it

BAIL IT IN—Feed the locomotive firebox

BAKE HEAD—Locomotive fireman. Also called bell ringer, blackie, and many other names scattered throughout this glossary

BALING-WIRE MECHANIC—A man of little mechanical ability

BALL OF FIRE—fast runs

BALLAST—Turkey or chicken dressing

BALLAST SCORCHER—Speedy engineer

BAND WAGON—Pay car or pay train from which wages were handed out to railroad employees

BANJO—Fireman's shovel; old-style banjo-shaped signal

BAREFOOT— A car or engine without brakes. (Many locomotives built in the 1860's and 1870's were not equipped with brakes except on the tank)

BARN—Locomotive roundhouse, so-called from the building in which streetcars are housed

BAT THE STACK OFF OF HER—Make fast time, work an engine at full stroke

BATTING 'EM OUT—Used generally by switchmen when a yard engine is switching a string of cars

BATTLESHIP— Large freight engine or interurban car, or a coal car. Also a formidable female, such as the landlady or a henpecked man's wife

BEANERY— Railroad eating house. Beanery queen is a waitress

BEANS—Meet orders; lunch period

BEAT 'ER ON THE BACK—Make fast time; work an engine at full stroke

BEEHIVE—Railroad yard office

BELL RINGER—Locomotive fireman

BEND THE IRON—Change the position of the rust a switch. Also called bend or bend the rail

BIG BOYS—Special trains for officials

BIG E—Engineer, so called from the large initial on membership buttons of the Brotherhood of Locomotive Engineers

BIG FOUR—the four operating Brotherhoods: Brotherhood of Railroad Trainmen, Order of Railway Conductors, Brotherhood of Locomotive Firemen and Enginemen, and Brotherhood of Locomotive Engineers

BIG HOLE—this was an emergency application of air-brake valve, causing a quick stop. Big-holing the train, the same as wiping the clock, is making an emergency stop

BIG HOOK— Wrecking crane

BIG O—Conductor; so named from first initial in Order of Railway Conductors. Sometimes called big ox and less complimentary terms

BIG ROCK CANDY MOUNTAINS—Hobo's paradise, as described in song by Harry K. McClintock. (See Indian Valley Line)

BINDERS—Hand brakes

BINDLE STIFF or BLANKET STIFF—Hobo who totes a blanket and uses it wherever night finds him. (Bindle is a corruption of "bundle")

BIRD CAGE—Brakeman's or switchman's lantern

BLACK DIAMONDS—Company coal. Diamond cracker is a locomotive fireman

BLACK HOLE—Tunnel

BLACK ONES—Railway Express refrigerator or boxcars having no interior illumination pressed into mail service during the Christmas rush

BLACK SNAKE—Solid train of loaded coal cars

BLACKBALLED—black-listed, boycotted

BLACKJACKS—Fifty-ton Santa Fe coal cars painted black

BLAZER—Hot journal with the packing afire

BLEED—Drain air from. Bleeder is valve by which air is bled from auxiliary reservoir of a car

BLIND BAGGAGE—Hobo riding head end of baggage car next to tender, where no door is placed; commonly called riding the blinds

BLIZZARD LIGHTS— Originally the lights on either side of the headlight that served in emergency when the oil-burning headlight blew out. Now they indicate the train is non-scheduled or extra train

BLOOD—Old-time engine built by Manchester Locomotive Works. Mr. Aretas Blood being the builder's name

BLOW 'ER DOWN—Reduce water in a locomotive boiler when carrying too much

BLOW SMOKE—Brag

BLOW UP—Use the blower to increase draft on the fire and thereby raise the steam pressure in the boiler. Also quit a job suddenly

'BO—Hobo. 'Bo chaser is freight brakeman or railroad policeman

BOARD—Fixed signal regulating railroad traffic, usually referred to as slow board, order board., clear board (for clear tracks) or red board (stop). Do not confuse this with extra board or spare board, colloquially known as slow board or starvation list, usually containing names of qualified train or enginemen not in regular active service that are called to work in emergencies. These names are listed in order of seniority; the man hired most recently being the last one called to service

BOBTAIL—Switch engine

BOILER ASCENSION—Boiler explosion

BOILER HEADER—Man riding in engine cab

BOILERS WASH—a high-water engineer

BOOK OF RULES—Examination based on facts in rulebook

BOOKKEEPER—Trainman who makes out reports; flagman

BOOTLEGGER—Train that runs over more than one railroad

BOOMER—Drifter who went from one railroad job to another, staying but a short time on each job or each road. This term dates back to pioneer days when men followed boom camps. The opposite is home guard. Boomers should not be confused with tramps, although they occasionally became tramps. Boomers were railroad workers often in big demand because of their wide experience, sometimes blackballed because their tenure of stay was uncertain. Their common practice was to follow the "rushes"-that is, to apply for seasonal jobs when and where they were most needed, when the movement of strawberry crops, watermelons, grain, etc., was making the railroads temporarily short-handed. There are virtually no boomers in North America today. When men are needed for seasonal jobs they are called from the extra board

BOUNCER—Caboose

BOWLING ALLEY— Hand-fired coal-burning locomotive. (A fireman throwing in the lumps of coal goes through motions that resemble bowling)

BOXCAR TOURIST—Hobo

BRAIN PLATE—Trainman's cap or hat badge

BRAINS or THE BRAINS—Conductor; sometimes called brainless wonder, a term also applied to any train or engineman or official who does things his fellows consider queer

BRAKE CLUB—Three-foot hickory stick used by freight trainmen to tighten hand brakes. Sometimes called sap or staff of ignorance

BRASS—A Babbitt-lined blank of bronze that forms the bearing upon which the car rests. To brass a car is to replace one of those bearings

BRASS BUTTONS—Passenger conductor on railroad or streetcar line

BRASS COLLAR or BRASS HAT— Railroad official. Term may have originated from gold-braided collar of conductor's uniform and brass plate on his cap

BRASS POUNDER—Telegraph operator

BREEZE—Service air

BRIDGE HOG—Bridge and building carpenter of the old school antedating steel and concrete

BROKEN KNUCKLES—Railroad sleeping quarters

BROWNIES— was demerits. This system is traced back to George R. Brown, general superintendent of the Fall Brook Railway (now part of the New York Central) in 1885. He thought the then current practice of suspending men for breaking rules was unfair to their families and substituted a system of demerit marks. Too many demerits in a given period resulted in dismissal. The Brown system, with many variations, has since been widely adopted by the railroad industry. A superintendent's private car is called brownie box or brownie wagon

BUCK THE BOARD—working the extra board. (See board)

BUCKLE THE RUBBERS—Connect air, steam, or signal hose

BUG—Telegraph instrument or trainman's or switchman's light, which is also called bug torch. Bug may also be a three-wheeled electric truck that carries mail and baggage around terminals

BUG LINE—Telephone connection between engine house and yard or telegraph office

BUG SLINGER—Switchman or brakeman

BUGGY—Caboose; rarely applied to other cars

BULL—Railroad policeman. Also called flatfoot or gumshoe, but the distinctive railroad terms are cinder dick and 'bo chaser

BULL PEN—Crew room

BULLGINE—Steam locomotive

BULLNOSE—Front drawbar of a locomotive

BUMP— Obtain another man's position by exercising seniority. When a crew is deprived of its assignment, as when a train is removed from the timetable, its members select the jobs they wish from those held by others with less whiskers

BUMPER—Post at end of spur track, placed there to stop rolling stock from running onto the ground

BUNCH OF THIEVES— Wrecking crew

BUST UP A CUT— To separate the cars in a train, removing some that have reached their destination, assigning others to through trains, etc.

BUTTERFLY—Note thrown (or handed) from train by an official to a section foreman or other employee, so called because it may flutter along the track, although it is usually weighted down when thrown from a car

BUZZARDS' ROOST—Yard office

CABOOSE BOUNCE, CABOOSE HOP— Early term for a train composed only of an engine and caboose

CAGE—Caboose

CALLER—One whose duty is to summon train or engine crews or announce trains

CALLIOPE—Steam locomotive

CAMEL or CAMELBACK—Engine with control cab built over middle of boiler, suggesting camel's hump. Also called Mother Hubbard type

CAN—Tank car

CANNED—Taken out of service

CAPTAIN—Conductor; often called skipper. This title dates from Civil War days when some railroads were run by the Army and the conductor was in many cases a captain

CAR-CATCHER—Rear brakeman

CAR KNOCKER— Car inspector or car repairer-from the early custom of tapping the wheels to detect flaws. Also called car whacker; and car toad (because he squats while inspecting), car tink, and car tonk

CAR-SEAL HAWK—Railroad policeman

CARD—Credentials showing Brotherhood or Union membership

CARHOUSE CAR—Covered cement car

CARRY A WHITE FEATHER—Show a plume of steam over the safety valves of the engine

CARRYING GREEN—Train whose engine displays green flags by day or green lights by night to indicate that a second section is following closely. Carrying white in the same manner signifies an extra train

CARRYING THE BANNER—Flagging. Also wearing ostentatious Brotherhood emblems, frequently done by 'bos in working the main stem for a handout

CARRYING THE MAIL—Bringing train orders

CASEY JONES—any locomotive engineer, especially a fast one. Name derived from John Luther (Casey) Jones

CATWALK— walkway on top of boxcars; sometimes called the deck from which comes the word deckorate

CHAIN GANG—Crew assigned to pool service, working first in, first out

CHAMBERMAID—Machinist in roundhouse

CHARIOT—Caboose, or general manager's car

CHASING THE RED—Flagman going back with red flag or light to protect his train

CHECKER—a company spy, particularly one checking up on loss of materials or of the receipts of an agent or conductor

CHERRY PICKER—Switchman, so called because of red lights on switch stands. Also any railroad man who is always figuring on the best jobs and sidestepping undesirable ones (based on the old allusion, "Life is a bowl of cherries")

CHEW CINDERS—Engines do this when reversed while running and while working quite a bit of steam

CHIP PIES—Narrow-gauge cars

CINDER CRUNCHER— Switchman or flagman. Cinder skipper is yard clerk

CINDER DICK—Railroad policeman or detective

CINDER SNAPPER—Passenger who rides open platforms on observation car

CIRCUS—Railroad

CLAW—Clinker hook used by fireman

CLEARANCE CARD—Authority to use main line

CLOCK— Steam gauge. (See wiping the clock; don't confuse with Dutch clock). Also fare register

CLOWN— Switchman or yard brakeman. Clown wagon is caboose

CLUB— Same as brake club. Club winder is switchman or brakeman. A brakeman's club was usually his only weapon of defense against hoboes

COAL HEAVER—Fireman, sometimes called stoker

COCK-LOFT— Cupola of a caboose. Also called crow's nest

COFFEE— Respite period enjoyed by baggage men while awaiting arrival of the next train. Also called spot

COFFEEPOT—little, old, steam locomotive

COLLAR AND ELBOW JOINT—Boardinghouse. (There isn't too much room at dinner table)

COLOR-BLIND—Employee who can't distinguish between his own money and the company's

COMPANY BIBLE—Book of rules

COMPANY JEWELRY—Trainman's hat, badge, and switch keys

COMPANY NOTCH or WALL STREET NOTCH— Forward corner of the reverse gear quadrant. It is called the company notch because an engine exerts full pulling power when worked with a full stroke

CONDUCER—Conductor

CONSIST—Contents or equipment of a train. Report form sent ahead so yardmaster can make plans for switching the train. The report is usually dropped off to an operator; this is dropping the consist

COOL A SPINDLE—Cool a hotbox by replacing the brass or putting water on the bearing

COON IT—Crawl

CORNERED—when a car, not in the clear on a siding, is struck by a train or engine

CORNFIELD MEET—Head-on collision or one that is narrowly averted

COULDN'T PULL A SETTING HEN OFF HER NEST—Derogatory description of old-fashioned locomotive

COUNTING THE TIES— Reducing speed

COW CAGE— a stock car. Also called cow crate

COWCATCHER— was a pilot. The old term was discarded by railroad officials, probably because it was a butt for jokesters. You've often heard about the passenger on a slow local train complaining to the conductor, "I don't understand why you have the cowcatcher on the front of the engine. This train can never overtake a cow. But if you'd attach it to the rear of the train it might at least discourage cows from climbing into the last car and annoying the passengers"

CRADLE—Gondola or other open-top car

CRIB—Caboose

CRIPPLE—See bad order

CROAKER—Company doctor

CROWNING HIM—Coupling a caboose on a freight train when it is made up

CRUMB BOSS—Man in charge of camp cars

CRUMMY— was the caboose. It is also called Crum box, crib and many other names. Innumerable poems have been written about "the little red caboose behind the train"

CUPOLA—Observation tower on caboose

CUSHIONS— Passenger cars. Cushion rider may be either a passenger or member of passenger-train crew. (See varnished cars)

CUT— Several cars attached to an engine or coupled together by themselves. Also that part of the right-of-way which is excavated out of a hill or mountain instead of running up over it or being tunneled through it

CUT THE BOARD—Lay off the most recently hired men on the extra list. (See board)

DANCING ON THE CARPET—called to an official's office for investigation or discipline

DEADBEAT— is defined by Webster as "one who persistently fails to pay his debts or way." The word was coined in the late 1800's when railroad workers noticed that loaded freight cars made a different beat over the track-joints than cars that weren't carrying a load. The empty cars made a "dead beat" which meant they weren't paying their way. By the beginning of the 20th century "deadbeat" came to encompassed people who failed to carry their share of the load also.

DEAD IRON and LIVE IRON—the two sets of tracks on a scale

DEAD MAN'S HOLE—Method of righting an overturned engine or car. A six-foot hole is dug about forty feet from the engine or car, long enough to hold a large solid-oak plank. A trench is then dug up to the engine and heavy ropes laid in it, with a four-sheave block, or pulley, at the lower end of the engine and a three-sheave block at the top of the boiler. Chains are fastened to the underside of the engine and hooked to the three-sheave block. The free end of the rope is then hooked to the drawbar of a road engine. The hole is filled-packed hard to hold the "dead man" down against the coming pull. When the engine moves up the track she pulls ropes over the top of the boiler of the overturned locomotive on the chains that are fastened to the lower part, rolling the engine over sidewise and onto her wheels again

DEAD MAN'S THROTTLE—Throttle that requires pressure of operator's hand or foot to prevent power shut-off and application of brakes. An engine so equipped would stop instantly if the operator fell dead. Also called dead man's button

DEADHEAD— Employee riding on a pass; any nonpaying passenger, a fireman's derisive term for head brakeman who rides in the cab of the engine, or a locomotive being hauled "dead" on a train

DECK—Front part of engine cab. Also catwalk on roofs of boxcars

DECKORATE—Get out on top of freight cars to set hand brakes or receive or transmit signals. Derived from deck

DEHORNED—Demoted or discharged

DETAINER or DELAYER—Train dispatcher

DIAMOND— Railroad crossover. Black diamond is coal

DIAMOND CRACKER or DIAMOND PUSHER—Locomotive fireman

* **DICK SCRATCHER**—Dispatcher

DIE GAME—Stall on a hill

DING-DONG—Gas or gas-electric coach, usually used on small roads or branch lines not important enough to support regular trains; name derived from sound of its bell. Sometimes called doodlebug

DINGER—Conductor (man who rings the bell)

DINKY— A switch engine without tender, used around back shop and roundhouse, or any small locomotive. Alsoa four-wheel trolley car

DIPLOMA—Clearance or service letter; fake service letter

DIRTY CAR—Storage car containing a varied assortment of mail and parcels that demand extra work in separating

DISHWASHERS—Engine wipers at roundhouse

DITCH— That part of the right-of-way that is lower than the roadbed. A derailed train is "in the ditch"

DOGCATCHERS—Crew sent out to relieve another that has been outlawed-that is, overtaken on the road by the sixteen-hour law, which is variously known as dog law, hog law, and pure-food law

DOGHOUSE—Caboose or its cupola

DONEGAN—Old car, with wheels removed, used as residence or office. Originated about 1900, when a Jersey Central carpenter and two foremen, all named Donegan, occupied three shacks in the same vicinity. People were directed to the Donegans so often that the shacks themselves came to be known by that name. The name stuck, even after the men had passed on and the shacks had been replaced by converted old cars

DONKEY—Derisive term for section man; small auxiliary engine

DOODLEBUG—Rail motorcar used by section men, linemen, etc. Also called ding dong

DOPE— Order, official instructions, explanation. Also a composition for cooling hot journals

DOPE IT—Use compound in the water to keep it from boiling when working an engine hard

DOPE MONKEY—Car inspector

DOUBLE—In going up a hill, to cut the train in half and take each section up separately

DOUBLE-HEADER—Train hauled by two engines

DOUSE THE GLIM— Extinguish a lantern, especially by a sudden upward movement

DRAG—Heavy train of "dead" freight; any slow freight train, as contrasted with manifest or hotshot

DRAWBAR FLAGGING— was a flagman leaning against the drawbar on the caboose, or standing near the caboose to protect the rear end of his train, instead of going back "a sufficient distance" as the rules require. Such a man is taking a chance, due maybe to laziness, exhaustion, severe cold, fear of the train leaving without him, etc.

DRIFTING THROTTLE— Running with steam throttle cracked open to keep air and dust from being sucked into steam cylinders

DRILL CREW—Yard crew. (See yard)

DRINK—Water for locomotive

DRONE CAGE—Private car

DROP— A switching movement in which cars are cut off from an engine and allowed to coast to their places. (See hump)

DROP A LITTLE RUN-FAST—Oil the engine

DROP 'ER DOWN—Pull reverse lever forward. Drop 'er in the corner means to make fast time, figuratively dropping the Johnson bar in one corner of the cab

DROPPER—Switchman riding a car on a hump

DROWNING IT OUT— Cooling an overheated journal

DRUMMER—Yard conductor

DRUNKARD—Late Saturday-night passenger train

DUCATS—Passenger conductor's hat checks

DUDE—Passenger conductor

DUDE WRANGLER—Passenger brakeman

DUMMY— Employees' train. Dummy locomotive is a switcher type having the boiler and running gear entirely housed, used occasionally for service in public streets

DUST-RAISER—Fireman (shoveling coal into firebox)

DUSTING HER OUT—putting sand through the fire door of an oil burner while working the engine hard; this cuts out the soot in the flues and makes the locomotive steam. Also known as giving the old girl a dose of salts

DUTCH CLOCK—Speed recorder

DUTCH DROP—rarely used method of bringing a car onto the main line from a spur. The engine heads into the spur, couples head-on to the car, and backs out. When the car is moving fast enough the engine is cut off, speeds up to get back on the main line before the car, then moves forward ahead of the junction between the main line and the spur so the car rolls out behind the engine

DYNAMITER—Car on which defective mechanism sends the brakes into full emergency when only a service application is made by the engineer. Also, a quick-action triple valve

EAGLE-EYE—Locomotive engineer

EASY SIGN—Signal indicating the train is to move slowly

END MAN—Rear brakeman on freight train

ELECTRIC OWL—Night operator

ELEPHANT CAR—Special car coupled behind locomotive to accommodate head brakeman

EXTRA BOARD—See board

EYE—Trackside signal

FAMILY DISTURBER—Pay car or pay train

FAN—Blower on a locomotive boiler

FIELD—Classification yard

FIELDER or FIELD MAN—Yard brakeman

FIGUREHEAD—Timekeeper

FIRE BOY—Locomotive fireman

FIRST READER—Conductor's train book

FISH WAGON—Gas-electric car or other motorcar equipped with an air horn (which sounds like a fishmonger's horn)

FISHTAIL—Semaphore blade, so called from its peculiar shape

FIST—Telegraph operator's handwriting. This script, in the days before telephones, typewriters, and teletypes, was characterized by its swiftness, its bold flowing curves which connected one word with another, and its legibility. Ops were proud of their penmanship

FIXED MAN—Switchman in a hump yard assigned to one certain post from which he rides cars being humped

FIXED SIGNAL—Derisive term for a student brakeman standing on a boxcar with his lamp out and a cinder in his eye

FLAG—Assumed name. Many a boomer worked under a flag, when his name was black-listed

FLAT— it was a flat car. Also called a car that has had the top blown off

FLAT WHEEL— Car wheel that has flat spots on the tread. Also applied to an employee who limps

FLIMSY— Train order. (Standard practice is to issue these on tissue paper to facilitate the making of carbon copies)

FLIP— To board a moving train. The word accurately suggests the motion used

FLOATER— Same as boomer

FLY LIGHT—Miss a meal. Boomers often did that; hoboes still do

FLYING SWITCH— A switching technique in which the engine pulls away from a car or cars she has started rolling, permitting them to be switched onto a track other than that taken by the engine. The switch is thrown instantly after the engine has passed it and just before the cars reach it. This procedure, common in bygone days, is now frowned upon by officials

FOG—Steam

FOOTBOARD— The step on the rear and front ends of switch or freight engines. Many casualties were caused in the "good old days" by switchmen missing these steps on dark slippery nights

FOOTBOARD YARD MASTER—Conductor who acts as yardmaster in a small yard

FOREIGN CAR—Car running over any railroad other than one that owns it

FOUNTAIN— That part of a locomotive where steam issues from the boiler and flows into pipes for lubrication, injection, etc.

FREEZE A HOB or A BLAZER—Cool a heated journal

FREEZER— A refrigerator car. Also reefer or riff

FROG—Implement for re railing cars or engines. Also an X-shaped plate where two tracks cross

FUSEE—Red flare used for flagging purposes. Its sharp point is driven into the right-of-way and no following train may pass as long as it is burning, although on some roads it is permissible to stop, extinguish the fusee, and proceed with caution in automatic block-signal limits

GALLOPER—Locomotive, the iron horse

GALLOPING GOOSE—A shaky section car

GALVANIZER—Car inspector

GANDY DANCER—Track laborer. Name may have originated from the gander-like rhythm of a man tamping ties, or from the old Gandy Manufacturing Company of Chicago, which made tamping bars, claw bars, picks, and shovels

GANGWAY—Space between the rear cab post of a locomotive and her tender

GARDEN—See yard

GAS HOUSE—Yard office

GATE—Switch

GAY CAT—Tramp held in contempt by fellow vagrants because he is willing to work if a job comes along

GENERAL—Yardmaster, abbreviated Y.M.

GET THE ROCKING CHAIR—Retire on a pension

GET YOUR HEAD CUT IN—Boomer slang for "wise up"

GIRL or OLD GIRL— Affectionate term for steam engine. The locomotive, like the sailing ship, is often called "she" instead of "it"

GIVE HER THE GRIT—Use sand

GLASS CARS—Passenger cars

GLIM—Switchman's or trainman's lantern

GLIMMER—Locomotive headlight

GLORY— String of empty cars. Also death, especially by accident

GLORY HUNTER—Reckless, fast-running engineer

GLORY ROAD—Sentimental term for railroad

GOAT— Yard engine. (See yard)

GOAT FEEDER—Yard fireman

GO HIGH—same as deckorate

G.M. — stands for General Manager. G.Y.M. is general yardmaster

GODS OF IRON—Huge, powerful locomotives

GON—Gondola, or steel-sided, flat-bottom coal car

GONE FISHING—Laid off

GOO-GOO EYE—Locomotive with two fire doors

GOOSE— To make an emergency stop

GOOSE HER—Reverse a locomotive that is under headway

GO-TO-HELL SIGNAL—Signal given with violent motion of hand or lantern

GRAB IRON—Steel bar attached to cars and engines as a hand bold

GRABBER—Conductor of passenger trains. (He grabs tickets)

GRAMOPHONE—Obsolete term for telephone

GRASS WAGON— was a tourist car. (Tourists like scenery)

GRASSHOPPER—Old type of locomotive with vertical boiler and cylinders

GRAVE-DIGGER—Section man

GRAVEYARD— Siding occupied by obsolete and disused engines and cars; scrap pile

GRAVEYARD WATCH—12.01 A.M. to 8 A.M., or any midnight shift, so called because that shift includes the quietest hours of the day

GRAZING TICKET—Meal book

GREASE MONKEY—Car oiler

GREASE THE PIG—Oil the engine. (See hog)

GREASY SPOON— Railroad eating house. Bill of fare is colloquially known as switch list, fork is hook, butter is grease pot, hotcakes are blind gaskets, and beans are torpedoes

GREENBACKS—Frogs for re-railing engines or cars

GREENBALL FREIGHT—Fruit or vegetables

GREEN EYE— Clear signal. (At the time Cy Warman wrote his celebrated poem, "I Hope the Lights Are White," the clear signal was white and green meant caution. This was changed years ago because of the fact that when a red or green signal lens broke or fell out it exposed a white, thus giving a clear board to engineers even though the signal itself was set to stop or go slow)

GREETINGS FROM THE DS—Train orders from the dispatcher

GRIEVER—Spokesman on grievance committee; Brotherhood or Union representative at an official investigation

GRIND—Shay-geared engine

GROUNDHOG—Brakeman, yardmaster, or switch engine

GRUNT— Locomotive engineer. Traveling grunt is road foreman of engines (hogs). Grunt may also be a lineman's ground helper; grunting is working as a lineman's helper

GUN—Torpedo, part of trainman's equipment; it is placed on the track as a signal to the engineer. Also, it is the injector on the locomotive that forces water from tank to boiler. To gun means to control air-brake system from rear of train

GUNBOAT—Large steel car

GUT—Air hose. Guts is drawbar

HACK—Caboose

HALF—Period of two weeks

HAM—Poor telegrapher or student

HAND BOMBER or HAND GRENADE—Engine without automatic stoker, which is hand-fired

HAND-ON—Train order or company mail caught with the hoop or without stopping

HANGING UP THE CLOCK—Boomer term that meant hocking your railroad watch

HARNESS—Passenger trainman's uniform

HASH HOUSE—Railroad restaurant or lunch stand

HAT— Ineffectual railroad man. (All he uses his head for is a hat rack)

HAY—Sleep on the job; any kind of sleep. Caboose was sometimes called hay wagon

HAY BURNER—Hand oil lantern, inspection torch. Also a horse used in railroad or streetcar service

HEAD-END REVENUE—Money which railroads receive for hauling mail, express, baggage, newspapers, and milk in cans, usually transported in cars nearest the locomotive, these commodities or shipments being known as head-end traffic

HEAD IN—Take a sidetrack when meeting an opposing train

HEAD MAN— Front brakeman on a freight train who rides the engine cab. Also called head pin

HEARSE—Caboose

HEEL—Cars on end of tracks with brakes applied

HERDER—Man who couples engines and takes them off upon arrival and departure of trains

HIGHBALL—Signal made by waving hand or lamp in a high, wide semicircle, meaning "Come ahead" or "Leave town" or "Pick up full speed." Verb highball or phrase 'ball the jack means to make a fast run. Word highball originated from old-time ball signal on post, raised aloft by pulley when track was clear. A very few of these are still in service, in New England and elsewhere

HIGHBALL ARTIST—A locomotive engineer known for fast running

HIGH-DADDY— Flying switch

HIGH IRON—Main line or high-speed track (which is laid with heavier rail than that used on unimportant branches or spurs)

HIGH LINER—Main-line fast passenger train

HIGH-WHEELER—Passenger engine or fast passenger train. Also highball artist

HIKER—A lineman who "hikes sticks" instead of prosaically climbing poles

HIT 'ER—Work an engine harder. (Was a variation of "hit the ball," which means, "Get busy-no more fooling around!"?)

HIT THE GRIT or GRAVEL—Fall off a car or locomotive or get kicked off

HOBO—Tramp. Term is said to have originated on Burlington Route as a corruption of "Hello, boy!" which construction workers used in greeting one another

HOG—Any large locomotive, usually freight. An engineer may be called a hogger, hoghead, hogmaster, hoggineer, hog jockey, hog eye, grunt, pig-mauler, etc. Some few engineers object to such designations as disrespectful, which they rarely are. For meaning of hog law see dogcatchers. Hoghead is said to have originated on the Denver & Rio Grande in 1887, being used to label a brakeman's caricature of an engineer

HOLDING HER AGAINST THE BRASS—Running electric car at full speed

HOLE—Passing track where one train pulls in to meet another

HOME GUARD—Employee who stays with one railroad, as contrasted with boomer. A homesteader is a boomer who gets married and settles down

HOOK—Wrecking crane or auxiliary

HOOK 'ER UP AND PULL HER TAIL— To set the reverse lever up on the quadrant and pull the throttle well out for high speed

HOPPER—Steel-sided car with a bottom that opens to allow unloading of coal, gravel, etc.

HOPTOAD—Derail

HORSE 'ER OVER—Reverse the engine. This is done by compressed air on modern locomotives, but in early days, manually operated reversing equipment required considerable jockeying to reverse an engine while in motion

HOSE COUPLER—Brakeman who handles trains by himself with the road engine around a big passenger terminal

HOSTLER— Any employee (usually a fireman) who services engines, especially at division points and terminals. Also called ash pit engineer

HOT— Having plenty of steam pressure (applied to locomotives)

HOT-FOOTER—Engineer or conductor in switching service who is always in a hurry

HOT JEWEL— Same as hotbox

HOT-WATER BOTTLE— Elesco feed water heater

HOT WORKER—Boilermaker who repairs leaks in the firebox or flue sheet while there is pressure in the boiler

HOTBOX—Overheated journal or bearing. Also called a hub. This was a frequent cause of delay in the old days but is virtually nonexistent on trains that are completely equipped with ball-bearings. Trainmen are sometimes called hotbox detectors

HOTSHOT—Fast train; frequently a freight made up of merchandise and perishables. Often called a manifest or red ball run

HOW MANY EMS HAVE YOU GOT? —How many thousand pounds of tonnage is your engine pulling? (M stands for 1,000)

HUMP—Artificial knoll at end of classification yard over which cars are pushed so that they can roll on their own momentum to separate tracks. (See drop.) Also, it is the summit of a hill division or the top of a prominent grade. Boomers generally referred to the Continental Divide as the Hump

HUMPBACK JOB— Local freight runs. (Conductor spends much time in caboose bending over his wheel reports)

HUT—Brakeman's shelter just back of the coal bunkers on the tender tank of engines operating through Moffat Tunnel. May also refer to caboose, locomotive cab, switchman's shanty, or crossing watchman's shelter

IDLER—an unloaded flatcar placed before or after a car from which oversize machinery, pipe, or other material projects

IN—A trainman who is at the home terminal and off duty is in

IN THE CLEAR—A train is in the clear when it has passed over a switch and frog so far that another train can pass without damage

IN THE COLOR—Train standing in the signal block waiting for a clear board

IN THE DITCH—Wrecked or derailed

IN THE HOLE— was on a siding. (See hole.) Also in the lower berth of a Pullman, as contrasted with on the tot, in the upper berth

INDIAN VALLEY LINE—An imaginary railroad "at the end of the rainbow," on which you could always find a good job and ideal working conditions. (It does not refer to the former twenty-one-mile railroad of that name between Paxton and Engels, Calif.) Boomers resigning or being fired would say they were going to the Indian Valley. The term is sometimes used to mean death or the railroader's Heaven. (See Big Rock Candy Mountains)

IND ICATORS—Illuminated signs on the engine and caboose that display the number of the train

IRON or RAIL—Track. Single iron means single track

IRON HORSE—Academic slang for locomotive

IRON SKULL— Boilermaker. (Jim Jeffries, one-time champion prize fighter, worked as an iron skull for years)

JACK— Locomotive. (A term often confused with the lifting device, hence seldom used)

JACKPOT— Miscellaneous assortment of mail and parcels piled in the aisle of a baggage car and requiring removal before the mail in the stalls can be "worked"

JAILHOUSE SPUDS—Waffled potatoes

JAM BUSTER—Assistant yardmaster

JAM NUTS—Doughnuts

JANNEY—to couple; derived from the Janney automatic coupler

JAWBONE SHACK—Switch shanty

JAY ROD—Clinker hook

JERK A DRINK—Take water from track pan without stopping train. From this came the word jerkwater, which usually means a locality serving only to supply water to the engines of passing trains; a Place other than a regular stop, hence of minor importance as jerkwater town, jerkwater college, etc.

JERK-BY—See flying switch

JERK SOUP—same as jerk a drink

JERRY—Section worker; sometimes applied to other laborers

JEWEL—Journal brass

JIGGER—Full tonnage of "dead" freight

JIMMIES—Four-wheel coal or ore cars

JITNEY— Four-wheel electric truck that carries baggage around inside a terminal. Also unregulated private automobile that carried passengers on public highways for 5-cent fare in direct competition with trolley cars

JOHNSON BAR— Reverse lever on a locomotive. (See drop 'er down)

JOIN THE BIRDS—Jump from moving engine or car, usually when a wreck is imminent

JOINT— A length of rail, generally 33 or 39 feet. Riding to a joint is bringing cars together so that they couple

JOKER— In dependent or locomotive brake, part of E-T (engine-train) equipment

JUGGLER—Member of way-freight crew who loads and unloads LCL freight at station stops

JUGGLING THE CIRCLE— Missing a train-order hoop

JUICE— was electricity. Juice fan is one who makes a hobby out of electric railways (juice lines)

JUNK PILE— Old worn-out locomotive that is still in service.

KANGAROO COURT—An official hearing or investigation, so named because it may be held wherever most convenient, anywhere along the road, jumping around like a kangaroo, to act on main-line mix ups or other urgent problems

KEELEY—Water can for hot journals or bearings. Nickname derived from "Keeley cure" for liquor habit

KETTLE—Any small locomotive, especially an old, leaky one. Also called teakettle and coffeepot

KEY—Telegraph instrument

KICK—See drop

KICKER—Triple valve in defective order, which throws air brakes into emergency when only a service application is intended, or sometimes by a bump of the train

KING— Freight conductor or yardmaster. King snipe is foreman of track gang. King pin is conductor

KITCHEN— Caboose; engine cab. Firebox is kitchen stove

* KNOCK HER IN THE HEAD—Slow Down

KNOCKOUT— Same as bump

KNOWLEDGE BOX—Yardmaster's office; president of the road

LADDER—Main track of yard from which individual tracks lead off. Also called a lead. (See yard)

LAPLANDER—Passenger jostled into someone else's lap in crowded car

LAST CALL, LAST TERMINAL, etc—Death

LAY-BY—Passing track, sidetrack. Laid out is delayed

LAY OVER—Time spent waiting for connection with other train

LCL—Less than carload lots of freight

LETTERS—Service letters given to men who resign or are discharged. Applicants for railroad jobs are usually asked to present letters proving previous employment. In the old days, when these were too unfavorable, many boomers used faked letters or would work under a flag on somebody else's certificates

LEVER JERKER—Interlocker lever man

LIBRARY— Cupola of caboose. Trainman occupying it was sometimes known as a librarian

LIFT TRANSPORTATION—Collect tickets

LIGHT ENGINE— An engine moving without cars attached

LIGHTNING SLINGER—Telegraph operator

LINER—Passenger train

LINK AND PIN—Old-time type of coupler; used to denote old fashioned methods of railroading

LIZARD SCORCHER—Dining-car chef

LOADS—Loaded freight cars

LOCAL LOAD—A truckload of mail in sacks and parcels sent from the storage car direct to a car on a local train, containing mail for towns along the route of the train

LOUSE CAGE—Caboose

LUNAR WHITE—The color of white used on all switches except on main line

LUNCH HOOKS— Your two hands

LUNG—Drawbar or air hose

LUNG DOCTOR— Locomotive engineer who pulls out drawbars. Also lung specialist

MADHOUSE— Engine foreman; scene of unusual activity or confusion MAIN IRON-Main track. Also called main stem MAIN PIN-An official MAKE A JOINT-Couple cars MANIFEST-Same as hotshot MARKERS-Signals on rear of train, flags by day and lamps by night MASTER MANIAC-Master mechanic, often abbreviated M.M. Oil is called master mechanic's blood

MASTER MIND— An official

MATCHING DIALS— Comparing time

MAUL—Work an 'engine with full stroke and full throttle

MEAT RUN—Fast run of perishable freight, hotshot

MEET ORDER—Train order specifying a definite location where two or more trains will meet on a single track, one on a siding, the others on the high iron

MERRY-GO-ROUND—Turntable

MIDDLE MAN, MIDDLE SWING— Second brakeman on freight train

MIKE—Mikado-type engine (2-8-2), so named because first of this type were built for Imperial Railways of Japan. (Because of the war with Japan, some railroads rechristened this type MacArthur)

MILEAGE HOG—Engineer or conductor, paid on mileage basis, who uses his seniority to the limit in getting good runs, which younger men resent

MILK TRUCK— Large hand truck with high cast-iron wheels used to transfer milk cans around in a terminal

MILL—Steam locomotive, or typewriter

MIXED LOAD—Truckload of mail sacks and parcels for many destinations sent from storage car to the yard (an outside platform) for further separation before forwarding

MONKEY— When a crew has been on duty sixteen hours and is caught out on the road, the monkey gets them and they are required by ICC rules to tie -up until a new crew comes. (See dogcatchers)

MONKEY MONEY— The pass of a passenger who is riding free

MONKEY MOTION— Walschaert or Baker valve gear on locomotive. Monkey house is caboose. Monkey suit is passenger trainman's uniform or any other smart-looking uniform. Monkey tail is back-up hose

MOONLIGHT MECHANIC—Night roundhouse foreman

MOPPING OFF—refers to escaping steam

MOTHER HUBBARD—See Camelback

MOTOR—Electric locomotive

MOUNTAIN PAY—Overtime

MOVING DIRT—Fireman shoveling coal into firebox

MOVING SPIRIT—Train dispatcher, more often called DS

MTYS—Empty cars

MUCKERS—Excavators in construction work

MUD CHICKENS— was a surveyor. Mud-hop is yard clerk, mud-shop his office

MUD SUCKER—A non-lifting injector

MUDHEN—A saturated locomotive, one that is not superheated

MULE SKINNER—Driver of mule cart

MUSIC MASTER—Paymaster

MUTT AND JEFF PUMP—Denver & Rio Grande locomotive with big air pump on right and small one on left

MUZZLE LOADER—Hand-fired locomotive

NEWS BUTCHER—was a peddler who sells magazines, candy, fruit, 'etc., in trains. Usually employed nowadays by Union News Co. Thomas A. Edison, the inventor was a news butcher in his youth and became deaf when a conductor boxed his ears for accidentally starting a fire while experimenting in a baggage car near Smith Creek, Mich.

NICKEL GRABBER—Streetcar conductor

NIGGERHEAD—Turret at top of locomotive boiler, over crown sheet, from which saturated steam is taken for operation of pumps, stoker, injectors, and headlight turbine

19 ORDER—Train order that does not have to be signed for. Operator can hand it on a hoop or delivery fork as the train slows down. (See 31 orders)

99—Failure to protect your train or to flag it

NO-BILL— Nonunion or non-brotherhood railroad worker. Also called non-air

NOSE ON—Couple on with head end of engine

NOSEBAG—Lunch carried to work. Put on the nosebag means to eat a meal

NUMBER DUMMY—Yard clerk or car clerk; also called number grabber

NUT SPLITTER or NUT BUSTER—Machinist

OILCAN—Tank car

OLD GIRL—Affectionate term for steam engine

OLD HAND—Experienced railroader. Also called old head

* OLD HEAD—Lots of Seniority

OLD MAN—Superintendent or general manager

OLE HOSS—Salvage warehouse, or freight on hand

ON THE ADVERTISED— According to schedule; right on time. Often called on the card (timecard) and sometimes on the cat hop

ON THE CARPET—Commoner version of dancing on the carpet

ON THE GROUND—On the ties, as a derailed train

ON THE SPOT— See spot

OP—Telegraph operator

OPEN-AIR NAVIGATOR—Hobo riding freight on top

OPEN THE GATE—Switch a train onto or off a siding. Close the gate means to close the switch after the train has passed it

O.R.C. — was a conductor. (See big O)

ORDER BOARD—See board

OS— On (train) sheet; to report a train by to dispatcher

OUT— When a trainman is at a point other than his home terminal, either on or off duty, he is out

OUTLAWED—See dogcatchers

OVER THE KNOLL— Getting up the hill

OVERLAP— Where two block signals control the same stretch of track OWL-Streetcar or train that runs late at night; almost anything having to do with night

PADDLE—Semaphore signal

PADDLE WHEEL—Narrow-gauge locomotive with driving boxes outside of the wheels

PAIR OF PLIERS—Conductor's punch

PALACE—Caboose

PAPER CAR—Baggage car for the transportation of newspapers exclusively

PAPERWEIGHT— Railroad clerk, office worker. Also called pencil pusher

PARLOR— was a caboose. Parlor man or parlor maid is hind brakeman or flagman on freight train

PASSING THE CROAKER—being examined by company doctor

PEAKED END—Head end of train. Also pointed or sharp end

PEANUT ROASTER—any small steam engine

PECK—Twenty minutes allowed for lunch

PEDDLE—to set out freight cars

PEDDLER—Local way-freight train

PELICAN POND—Place outside a roundhouse (down South) where there is much ooze and slime, caused by the fact that many locomotives are run thirty days without the boilers being washed out. The boilers are kept clean by blowing them out with blow off cocks

PENNSYLVANIA—Coal

PERSUADER—Blower (for locomotive fire)

PETTICOAT— Portion of the exhaust stack that guides exhausted steam into the stack proper. When this becomes displaced, the spent steam goes back through the flues, cutting off the draft from the fire

PIE-CARD—was a meal ticket. Also called grazing ticket

PIG—was a locomotive. Pig-mauler is locomotive engineer; pigpen locomotive roundhouse. (See hog)

PIKE—Railroad

PIN AHEAD AND PICK UP TWO BEHIND ONE—Cut off the engine, pick up three cars from siding, put two on the train, and set the first one back on the siding

PIN FOR HOME—Go home for the day

PINHEAD— was a brakeman. Pin-lifter is yard brakeman. Pinner is a switchman that follows. Pin-puller is a switchman that cuts off cars from a train. The old-style link-and-pin coupler (now rarely used) was called Lincoln pin

PINK—Caution card or rush telegram

PLANT—Inter-locking system

PLUG—"One-horse" passenger train. Also throttle of old-style locomotive; hence engineers were known as plug-pullers. Plugging her means to use the reverse lever as a brake instead of the air. Local passenger trains are sometimes referred to as Plug runs.

PLUSH RUN—Passenger train

POCATELLO YARDMASTER—Derisive term for boomers, all of whom presumably claimed to have held, at some time, the tough job of night yardmaster at Pocatello, Idaho

POLE— Is to run light. (See light)

POLE PIN—Superintendent of telegraph

POP—To let safety valve on boiler release, causing waste of steam, making a loud noise, and, when engine is working hard, raising water in boiler, thereby causing locomotive to work water

POP CAR—Gasoline car or speeder, used by section men, linemen, etc.; so called because of the put-put noise of its motor exhaust

POPS—Retainers

POSITIVE BLOCK—Locomotive engineer

POSSUM BELLY—Toolbox under a caboose or under some wrecking cars

POUND HER—Work a locomotive to its full capacity

POUNDING THEIR EARS— Sleeping, making hay.

PUD— Pickup and delivery service

PULLER—Switch engine hauling cars from one yard to another at the same terminal. Also the operator of an electric truck that transfers baggage and mail around a terminal

PULL FREIGHT— To leave or to give up a job

PULL THE AIR—Set brakes by opening conductor's valve or angle cock

PULL THE CALF'S TAIL—Yank the whistle cord

PULL THE PIN— Uncouple a car by pulling up the coupling pin, or an expression meaning to resign or quit a job.

PURE-FOOD LAW—See dogcatchers

PUSHER—Extra engine on rear of train, usually placed there to assist in climbing a grade

PUSSYFOOTER—Railroad policeman

PUT 'ER ON—Make a reduction in air in the train's braking system. Put 'er all on means apply emergency brake, more commonly described as big-holing her

PUT ON THE NOSEBAG— Eat a meal

QUILL—Whistle (term used especially in the South)

QUILLING—Personalized technique of blowing a locomotive whistle, applicable only in the days before the whistles became standardized

RABBIT— A derail; an arrangement for preventing serious wrecks by sidetracking runaway trains, cars, or locomotives on a downgrade. Unlike regular sidetracks, the derail ends relatively abruptly on flat trackless land instead of curving back onto the main line. The term rabbit is applied to this device because of the timidity involved

RACE TRACK—Straight and flat stretch of track upon which an engineer can safely make unusually high speed. Also parallel stretches of track of two competing railroads upon which rival trains race one another (contrary to company rules but much to the delight of enginemen, trainmen, and passengers, and perhaps to the secret delight of some officials)

RAG-WAVER—Flagman

RAIL— Any railroad employee

RAILFAN— Anyone who makes a hobby of railroading

RAP THE STACK—Give your locomotive a wide-open throttle, make more speed. Rapper is an engineer who works his engine too hard

RATTLE HER HOCKS—Get speed out of an engine

RATTLER—Freight train

RAWHIDER—Official, or any employee, who is especially hard on men or equipment, or both, with which he works. A rawhider, or slave driver, delights in causing someone to do more than his share of work. Running too fast when picking up a man on the footboard, or making a quick stop just short of him when he is expecting to step on, so that he has to walk back, are two ways it is done; but there are almost as many ways of raw hiding as there are different situations

REAL ESTATE—Poor coal mixed with dirt or slag. When mixed with sand it is called seashore

RED BOARD—Stop signal

REDBALL, BALL OF FIRE—Fast freight train,

REDCAP—Station porter. Term coined about 1900 by George H. Daniels, New York Central publicist

RED EYE— Same as red board; also liquor

RED ONION— Eating house or sleeping quarters for railroad men

REEFER or RIFF—Refrigerator car

REPTILE—See snake

RETAINER—Small valve located near brake wheel for drawing off and holding air on cars. (Retainers often figure prominently in true tales and fiction stories about runaway cars on trains)

RIDIN' 'EM HIGH— Traveling on tops of boxcars, or going fast.

RIDIN' THE RODS—an old-time hobo practice, now virtually obsolete. The hobo would place a board across truss rods under a car and ride on it. This was very dangerous even in pleasant weather, and the possibility was ever present that you might doze, get careless, become too cramped, or lose your nerve-and roll under the wheels

RIDING THE POINT—Riding a locomotive, point referring to shape of pilot

RIGHT-HAND SIDE— Engineer's side of cab (on nearly all North American roads). Left-hand side is fireman's side. When a fireman is promoted he is set up to the right-hand side

RINGMASTER—Yardmaster

RIPRAP—Loose pieces of heavy stone or masonry used in some places to protect roadbeds from water erosion

RIP-TRACK— Minor repair track or car-repair department. RIP means repair

RIVET BUSTER—Boilermaker

ROAD HOG—any large motor vehicle on a highway, especially intercity trailer trucks and busses that cut into railroad freight and passenger revenue

ROOFED—Caught in close clearance

ROOF GARDEN— Mallet-type locomotive or any helper engine on a mountain job, also, sometimes called sacred ox.

ROUGHNECK—Freight brakeman

RUBBERNECK CAR—Observation car

RULE G—"The use of intoxicants or narcotics is prohibited"—one of twelve general rules in standard code adopted by Association of American Railroads, based upon previous regulations made by individual companies. Countless thousands of railroad men, especially boomers, have been discharged for violation of Rule G; not because of railroads' objection to liquor itself but because a man under the influence of liquor is not to be trusted in a job involving human lives and property

RUN— The train to which a man is assigned is his run

RUN-AROUND— If it is a man's turn to work and he is not called, he may claim pay for the work he missed. He has been given the run-around. A person below him on the list goes out ahead of him.

RUN-IN—A collision; an argument or fight

RUN LIGHT—for an engine to run on the tracks without any cars

RUNNER—Locomotive engineer

RUNT—Dwarf signal

RUST or STREAK O' RUST—Railroad

RUST PILE—Old locomotive

RUSTLING THE BUMS— Searching a freight train for hobos. In bygone days it was common practice for trainmen to collect money from freight-riding 'bos, often at the rate of a dollar a division.

SADDLE—First stop of freight car, under the lowest grab iron

SANDHOG—Laborer who works in a caisson tunneling under a river, boring either a railroad tunnel, subway, or highway tunnel

SAP—same as brake club; also called the staff of ignorance. To set hand brakes is to sap up some binders

SAWBONES—Company doctor

SAW BY—Slow complicated operation whereby one train passes another on a single-track railroad when the other is on a siding too short to hold the entire train. Saw by is applied to any move through switches or through connecting switches that is necessitated by one train passing another

SCAB—Nonunion workman; also car not equipped with automatic air system. (See non-air)

SCIZZOR-BILL—Uncomplimentary term referring to yard or road brakemen and students in train service

SCOOP—was a fireman's shovel. Also the step on front and rear ends of switch engines

SCOOT—Shuttle train

SCRAP PILE—Worn-out locomotive that is still in service

SEAT HOG—Passenger who monopolizes more than one seat in a car or station waiting room while others are standing. Such pests usually spread luggage, packages, or lunch over adjacent seats

SEASHORE—Sand used in sand dome. Also applied to coal that is mixed with sand

SECRET WORKS—Automatic air-brake application. Also the draft timbers and drawbar of a car, when extracted by force. If only the drawbar is pulled out, you say, "We got a lung," but if the draft timbers come with it, you say, "We got the whole damn secret works"

SENIORITY GRABBER—Railroad employee who is glad when someone above him dies, gets killed, is fired, or resigns, so he can move up the seniority list to a better job

SEPARATION—the sorting of mail sacks and parcels within the storage car before transferring to trucks

SERVICE APPLICATION—Gradual speed reduction, as contrasted with emergency stop caused by wiping the clock

SETTING UP—Loading a baggage car with mail and parcels according to a prearranged plan to facilitate rapid unloading at various stations along the line

SETUP—Four to six hand trucks placed in formation beside the door of a storage car to facilitate the separation of the mail and parcels being unloaded. Each truck is loaded with matter to be transferred to other trains or to the R.P.O. (Railway Post Office) terminal office

SHACK— Brakeman, occupant of caboose. Shacks master is a conductor SHAKE 'EM UP-Switching

SHAKING THE TRAIN— Putting on air brakes in emergency

SHANTY—Caboose

SHINER—Brakeman's or switchman's lantern

SHINING TIME— was starting time (probably from old Negro spiritual "Rise and Shine")

SHOO-FLY—Temporary track, usually built around a flooded area, a wreck, or other obstacle; sometimes built merely to facilitate a re-railing.

SHORT FLAGGING— Flagman not far enough from his train to protect it. (See drawbar flagging)

SHORT LOADS—Cars consigned to points between division points and set out on sidings at their destinations. Also called shorts

SHORT-TIME CREW—Crew working overtime but not yet affected by the sixteen-hour law. (See dogcatchers)

SHUFFLE THE DECK—Switch cars onto house tracks at every station you pass on your run

SHUNTING BOILER—switch engine

SIDE-DOOR PULLMAN—Boxcar used by hobos in stealing rides

SKATE—Shoe placed on rail in hump yard to stop cars with defective brakes

SKIN YOUR EYE—Engineer's warning to man on left side of cab when approaching curve

SKIPPER—Conductor

SKYROCKETS—Red-hot cinders from smokestack

SLAVE DRIVER— was the yardmaster. Also any rawhide.

SLING MORSE—Work as telegraph operator

SLIPS, CAR OR TRAIN OF—Car or train of bananas

SLOW BOARD—See board

SLUG—Heavy fire in locomotive firebox

SLUGS—A shipment of magazines, catalogues, or automobile-license plates in small mail sacks weighing approximately 100 pounds each

SMART ALECK—Passenger conductor

SMOKE or SMOKE AGENT—Locomotive fireman. Smoker is engine or firebox. Smoking 'em or running on smoke orders is a dangerous method, now obsolete, of running a train from one station or siding to another without orders from the dispatcher. You moved cautiously, continually watching for the smoke of any train that might be approaching you on the same track

SNAKE—Switchman, so named from the large serpentine letter S on membership pins of the Switchman's Union of North America. Sometimes called reptile or serpent

SNAKEHEAD—A rail that comes loose from the ties and pierces the floor of a car; a fairly common accident with the strap-iron rails of a century ago

SNAP—Push or pull with another engine. Snapper is the engine that does the pulling

SNIPE—Track laborer. His boss is a king snipe

SNOOZER—Pullman sleeping car

SNUFF DIPPERS—Coal-burning engines that burn lignite (which, on the Missouri Pacific at least, is the same color as snuff)

SOAK—Saturated locomotive

SODA JERKER—Locomotive fireman

SOFT BELLIES—Wooden frame cars

SOFT-DIAMOND SPECIAL—Coal train

SOFT PLUG—Fusible plug in crown sheet of locomotive that is supposed to drop when water gets below top of sheet

SOLID CAR—A completely filled storage car containing sixty feet of mail and parcels, equal to a 100 per cent load

SOLID TRACK—Track full of cars

SPAR—Pole used to shove cars into the clear when switching. (See stake)

SPEED GAUGER—Locomotive engineer

SPEEDER— Same as pop car

SPEEDY—Callboy

SPIKE A TORCH—Throw a fusee

SPOT— was to place a car in a designated position, also, sleep, rest, or lunch period on company time. On the spot means an opportunity for railroad men to "chew the rag" or swap experiences. Unlike the same underworld term, on the spot has no sinister implication in railroad slang. Spot time.

SPOTBOARD—Guide used by section men in surfacing or ballasting track in order to obtain an even bed.

SPOTTER—Spy, company man assigned to snoop around and check on employees

SQUEEZERS—Car-retarding system used in some railroad yards

SQUIRRELING— Climbing a car

STACK O' RUST—A locomotive that has seen better days

STAKE—Pole used in dangerous and now rare method of switching. A cut of cars was shoved by a stake attached to the car immediately in front of the engine. This method was supposed to be superior to the ordinary method of "batting them out" because there was less wear and tear on drawbars and less damage to freight; but the human casualties that resulted gave more than one yard the nickname "slaughterhouse." Another meaning of stake is the money a boomer saved on a job so he could resign and continue eating regularly while looking for another job

STAKE DRIVER— Any engineering-department man

STALL—Space inside a mail or baggage car containing mail or parcels consigned to a certain destination and separated from other shipments by removable steel posts

STARGAZER—Brakeman who fails to see signals

STARVATION DIET—See board

STEM—Track or right-of-way

STEM-WINDER—Climax type of geared locomotive. Also applied to trolley car without brakes because of the motion of its brake handle

STICK—Staff used on certain stretches of track to control the block. It is carried by engine crews from one station to another. Now rare

STIFF BUGGY— Specially designed four-wheel truck used for transferring coffins and rough boxes inside a station

STINGER — A brakeman. Derived from initial B(bee) of Brotherhood of Railroad Trainmen, or perhaps from some brakemen's habit of arousing hobos by applying a brake club to the soles of their shoes

STINK BUGGY—Bus

STINKER—Hotbox

STIRRUP—First step of freight car, under the lowest grab iron

STOCK PEN—Yard office

STOCKHOLDER— Any employee who is always looking out for the company's interests

STOPPER PULLER—Member of the crew that follows the engine in switching

STORAGE CAR—Baggage car or (in rush periods) Railway Express car containing a mixed shipment of parcels and mail sacks consigned to a certain terminal for sorting and rerouting to various destinations via other trains

STRAW BOSS—Foreman of small gang or acting foreman

STRAW-HAT BOYS—Railroad men who work only in pleasant weather

STRAWBERRY PATCH—Rear end of caboose by night; also railroad yard studded with red lights

STRETCH 'EM OUT—Take out slack in couplings and drawbars of train

STRING— Several cars coupled together; also a telegraph wire

STRUGGLE FOR LIFE—Existence in railroad boardinghouse

STUDE TALLOW—Student fireman

STUDENT—Learner in either telegraph, train, or engine service; an apprentice

SUCK IT BY—Make a flying switch

SUGAR—Sand

SUPER—Superintendent

SWELLHEAD—Conductor or locomotive engineer

SWING A BUG—Make a good job of braking. (See bug)

SWING MAN— Same as middle man

SWITCH LIST—Bill of fare at railroad eating house

SWITCH MONKEY—Switchman

TAIL OVER HER BACK—Engine with full head of steam, with plume resembling a squirrel's tail from her safety valve

TAKE THE RUBBER OUT OF THEM— Disconnect the air hoses on a train

TAKING YOUR MINUTES— stopping for lunch

TALLOWPOT— Locomotive fireman, so called from melted tallow used to lubricate valves and shine the engine

TANK— Locomotive tender. Tanker is tank car used in hauling oil, water, milk, chemicals or some other liquid

TEAKETTLE—See kettle

TEASE THE BRUTE—Follow the engine

TELLTALES—Any device that serves as a warning. Specifically the row of strips hanging down a short distance in front of a tunnel or low bridge to inform trainmen who are riding car tops that they'd better duck

* TEMPLE OF KNOWLEGE—Term for caboose

TERMINAL—Railway Post Office unit, usually at or near the railroad station, where mail is removed from sacks, sorted, and forwarded to its ultimate destination

TERMINAL LOAD—a shipment of mail consigned to a certain R.P.O. terminal office for sorting and reshipment in other sacks

THE BISCUITS HANG HIGH—there's a scarcity of food handouts in that locality.

THIRTY—Telegraphic term for "that's all-no more"

31 ORDER—Train order that must be signed for; the train must stop to pick it up. (See 19 orders)

THOUSAND-MILER—Black satin or blue percale shirt worn by railroaders, expected to last 1,000 miles between washings. (The usual basis of a day's work was about 100 miles, so two shirts could easily last from one pay day to the next)

THREE-BAGGER—Train pushed or pulled by three engines. (No doubt originated by a baseball fan)

THROTTLE-JERKER—Engineer

* THROTTLE GOD—Locomotive Engineer

THROW AWAY THE DIAMONDS—Term applied to locomotive fireman missing the fire door with a shovelful of coal and spilling some

* THROW OUT THE ANCHOR—Done for the Day

TIE 'EM DOWN—Set handbrakes

TIE ON—Couple on. Tie 'em together is to couple cars

TIE UP—Stop for a meal or for rest

TIER—Pile of mail sacks or parcels occupying the full width at each end of a car

TIMKENIZED—Equipped with Timken roller bearings

TIN LIZARD—Streamlined train

TING-A-LING—Small engine with "tinny" bell

TISSUE—Train order. (See flimsy)

TOAD—Derail. (See rabbit)

TOEPATH or TOWPATH—Running board of locomotive or catwalk on top of boxcars, or that part of railroad embankment lying between end of ties and shoulders of fill

TONK—Car repairer

TONNAGE HOUND or Hog—Trainmaster or other official who insists upon longer or heavier trains than the crew and motive power can handle efficiently

TOP DRESSER DRAWER—Upper bunk in caboose

TOWER BUFF—Rail fan so zealous that he disregards signs such as "Private," "No Admittance" and "Stay Out" on interlocking towers and other railroad structures

TRAIN LINE—Pipe that carries compressed air to operate air brakes

TRAMPIFIED—It is the way a boomer looked after being out of work a long time. His clothes were "ragged as a barrel of sauerkraut" and he needed a "dime's worth of decency" (shave)

TRAVELING CARD—Card given by a railroad Brotherhood to a man in search of employment. Also an empty slip bill

TRAVELING GRUNT—Road foreman of engines, traveling engineer. Sometimes called traveling man

TRICK—Shift, hours of duty

TRIMMER—Engine working in hump yard that goes down into yard and picks out misdirected cars and shoves them to clear. (See yard and hump)

TWO-WHEELER—Two-wheeled hand truck for transferring baggage and mail around in a station

UNCLE SAM—Railway Post Office clerk

UNDER THE TABLE—Just as a man who "can't take his liquor" is sometimes actually under the table, so, figuratively, is a telegraph operator when messages are being sent to him faster than he can receive

UNDERGROUND HOG—Chief engineer

UNLOAD—Get off train hurriedly

VARNISH—Passenger trains. Also called varnished shot, varnished job, varnished boxes, string of varnish, varnished wagons, etc. These nicknames are rarely applied to modern streamliners

VASELINE—Oil

* **VOODOO BARGE**—Updated Heavy, Slow Freight

WABASH—was to hit cars going into adjacent tracks. (See cornered) Also refers to the officially frowned-upon practice of slowing up for a stop signal at a crossing with another railroad instead of stopping. The engineer would look up and down to make sure everything is safe, and then start up again, having saved several minutes by not stopping entirely. Wabash may also mean a heavy fire in the locomotive firebox

WAGON— A railroad car. (English term)

WALK THE DOG—Wheel a freight train so fast as to make cars sway from side to side

WALK UP AGAINST THE GUN— Ascend a steep grade with the injector on

WALL STREET NOTCH—Forward corner of reverse lever quadrant in engine cab (more commonly called company notch). Called Wall Street notch because engine pays dividends when heaviness of train requires engine to be worked that way

WASHOUT—Stop signal, waved violently by using both arms and swinging them in downward arc by day, or swinging lamp in wide low semicircle across tracks at night

WATCH YOUR PINS—Be careful around stacks of ties, rails, etc.

WAY CAR—Caboose, or car of local freight

WEARING THE BLUE— Delayed by car inspectors. A blue flag or blue light is placed on cars thus delayed and being worked on

WEARING THE GREEN— Carrying green signals. When trains run in more than one section, all except the last must display two green flags

WEED BENDER—Railroaders' derisive term for cowboy, other such terms being hay shaker, clover picker, and plow jockey. Commonest term for cowboy is cowpuncher, which is of railroad origin. Cowboys riding stock trains prod the cattle

* WEED WEASEL—Company Official Spying on Crews

WESTINGHOUSE—Air brake, also called windjammer

WET MULE IN THE FIREBOX— Bad job of firing a locomotive

WHALE BELLY— is a steel car or type of coal car with drop bottom. Also called sow belly.

WHEEL 'EM—Let a train run without braking. Wheeling means carrying or hauling at good speed; also called highballing. You say wheeling the berries when you mean hauling the berry crop at high speed

WHEEL MONKEY—Car inspector

WHEN DO YOU SHINE? —What time were you called for?

WHISKERS—Quite a bit of seniority

WHISTLE OUT A FLAG—Engineer blows one long and three short blasts for the brakeman to protect rear of train

WHITE FEATHER—Plume of steam over safety valves, indicating high boiler pressure

WHITE RIBBONS—White flags (an extra train)

WHITEWASH—Milk

WIDEN ON HER—Open the throttle, increase speed

WIGWAG—A grade-crossing signal

WILLIE—Waybill for loaded car

WIND—Air brakes

WING HER—Set brakes on moving train

WISE GUY—Station agent

WOLF or LONE WOLF—Non-brotherhood man

WORKING A CAR—unloading a storage mail car

WORKING MAIL—Mail in sacks and pouches consigned to R.P.O. (Railway Post Office) cars to be "worked" or sorted in transit

WORK WATER—some old-time engineers preferred to work the water (operates the injector and watches the water glass or gauge cocks). On most roads, the fireman now works the water

WRECKING CREW—Relief crew. Derogatory term derived from the difficulty regular men sometimes experience in rearranging a car after it has been used by relief men

WRONG IRON—Main track on which the current of traffic is in the opposite direction

WYE—Tracks running off the main line or lead, forming a letter Y; used for turning cars and engines where no turntable is available

X—Empty car

XXX—the same as a bad order

YARD— System of tracks for making up trains or storing cars. (Boomer's version: "System of rust surrounded by a fence and inhabited by a dumb bunch of natives who will not let a train in or out.") It is also called a garden and field. Yard geese are yard switchmen. Y.M. is yardmaster. Yard goat is switching engine

ZOO KEEPER—Gate tender at passenger station

ZULU—Emigrant family with its household goods and farm equipment traveling by rail; sometimes included even livestock crowded into the same boxcar. Zulu can mean only the car, or the car and all its contents. This method of travel was not uncommon in homesteading days on Western prairies. Origin of term is obscure. May have some connection with the fact that British homesteaders in Africa fled in overfilled farm wagons before Zulu marauders

Index